SAINT HYACINTH
OF
POLAND

SAINT HYACINTH
OF
POLAND

THE STORY OF
THE APOSTLE OF THE NORTH

By
Mary Fabyan Windeatt

Illustrated by
Sister Mary of the Compassion, O.P.

TAN BOOKS AND PUBLISHERS, INC.
Rockford, Illinois 61105

Nihil Obstat: Arthur J. Scanlan, S.T.D.
                   Censor Librorum

Imprimatur: ✠ Francis J. Spellman, D.D.
                   Archbishop of New York
                   New York
                   July 1, 1945

First published in 1945, by Sheed & Ward, under the title *Northern Lights: The Story of Saint Hyacinth of Poland and His Companions.*

This book first appeared in serial form in the pages of *The Torch.*

ISBN: 0-89555-422-4

Library of Congress Catalog Card No.: 93-83094

Printed and bound in the United States of America.

TAN BOOKS AND PUBLISHERS, INC.
P.O. Box 424
Rockford, Illinois 61105

1993

To the memory
of my Father,
William Fabyan Windeatt.

CONTENTS

ABOUT THE ILLUSTRATOR

Sister Mary of the Compassion, O.P. (Constance Mary Rowe) was born in London. At the age of 15 she began to study art at the Clapham School of Art, and four years later became a student of the Royal College of Art, in London. There she made mural painting her principal aim, working under Sir William Rothenstein, Alfred K. Lawrence and Professor W. Tristram.

The question of "What is 'Good' and what is 'Evil,'" together with the conviction that the human soul was made to attain to the perfection of all truth, led her to the Catholic Church. She was baptized at the Brompton Oratory in September, 1931 and became a Dominican Tertiary in December of the same year. In 1932 she was awarded the Rome Prize for mural paintings, and her time as a student of the British School at Rome was spent in the study of painting in relation to its use in the Church.

Coming to America in 1936, she held exhibitions in New York, Washington, Boston and Providence. In 1937 she entered the cloister of the Dominican Sisters of the Perpetual Rosary, Union City, New Jersey.

ACKNOWLEDGMENTS

For the use of books and other material relative to the life and times of Saint Hyacinth, the author wishes to thank the following:

The Dominican Fathers of Saint Vincent Ferrer's Priory in New York City; the Fathers of the Dominican House of Studies in River Forest, Illinois; the Fathers of the Dominican Priory in St. Hyacinthe, Quebec, Canada.

Grateful acknowledgment is also due Mrs. Rose Lang of Brooklyn, New York, and Miss Jane Emmet of New York City, for their aid in translating much valuable source material, and to the Felician Sisters of the Academy of the Immaculate Heart of Mary in Buffalo, New York—in particular to Sister Mary Benice, Sister Mary Annette, Sister Mary Amandine and Sister Mary Gualbert—for their criticism and suggestions regarding the historical and geographical aspects of this story.

The author is also deeply indebted to the Reverend Norbert F. Georges, O.P., S.T.Lr., Director of the Blessed Martin Guild, for his unfailing help and encouragement in preparing this first English biography of Saint Hyacinth of Poland.

SAINT HYACINTH
OF
POLAND

CHAPTER 1

FOUR APOSTLES

IT WAS Ash Wednesday in the year 1220, but the city of Rome was far from being in a Lenten mood. A spirit of exhilaration was abroad that did not correspond to sackcloth or ashes. Indeed, one might have thought it already Easter, especially if one looked at the joyful countenance of Stephen Cardinal Orsini. The old man was radiant.

"Napoleon! My young nephew Napoleon!" he kept repeating every few minutes. "A little while ago the lad was dead, but now he lives!"

Nicholas, the Cardinal Bishop of Tusculum, smiled. He had been present that morning at the Monastery of Saint Sixtus when the news had been brought that Napoleon had been thrown from his horse and killed. Others had been present, too, for this was a great day in the Eternal City. Several communities of nuns, heretofore living without cloister, had agreed to band together at the Monastery of Saint Sixtus under the Rule drawn up for them by the holy Spanish preacher Dominic de Guzman. All had been assembled for Mass and the

1

solemn ceremony of inclosure when the messenger had rushed in.

Recalling all these things now, the Cardinal Bishop of Tusculum looked closely at his old friend. "If I live for a hundred years, I'll never forget this morning's miracle!" he declared. "Your nephew was really dead, Stephen. Anyone could see that. But this Spanish friar. . .this Father Dominic. . . why, he was not at all alarmed. He comforted you a little, of course—but even I could tell that his thoughts were far away from the tragedy."

Cardinal Stephen nodded. "Yes, I know. Instead of being distracted, like the rest of us, he went ahead and offered the Holy Sacrifice. When all was over, he came to where Napoleon's body was stretched on the floor. Then—oh, Nicholas! What wonderful words he spoke!"

Cardinal Nicholas was silent for a moment, remembering how the Spanish friar had knelt beside the broken body of the young man and arranged the shattered limbs; how finally he had arisen, made the Sign of the Cross, then looked heavenwards and cried out joyfully:

"Young man, I say to you, in the Name of Our Lord Jesus Christ, arise!"

Nicholas stretched out a reassuring hand to his old friend. "It has been a wonderful day," he murmured. "And one to remember forever, Stephen. For we have seen a saint at prayer and at work."

In a large house at some blocks' distance from where the two Italian Cardinals sat talking, other men were also discussing the morning's miracle.

These men were of a different build and coloring from the Cardinals, however—tall and muscular, with the fair hair and blue eyes that bespoke their Polish birth. The oldest, Ivo Odrowatz, wore the scarlet robes of a Bishop. He was seated in a large chair, with writing materials spread out on a table before him, while at his side stood two young priests, Hyacinth and Ceslaus, his nephews.

"We must try to see this Father Dominic before we go back to Poland," remarked the Bishop. "Oh, my sons! Pray, pray very hard that God will grant us the grace to speak with a man who can raise the dead to life!"

A soft glow stole into Hyacinth's eyes. "Maybe we should also pray for another favor," he suggested. "What do you think, Uncle Ivo? Could you use some of Father Dominic's friars in Cracow?"

"Of course we could use them!" put in Ceslaus eagerly. "What a wonderful idea!"

The Bishop's eyes turned from one young face to the other, and a little smile flickered on his lips. "Would you joke at such a time?" he asked. "If I thought that there was the least chance. . ."

"Put it in the letter, Uncle Ivo. Ask Father Dominic to give us some of his friars, so that northern Europe may be converted. Ask him this now— at the same time you ask for the privilege of an interview."

There was a respectful insistence in Hyacinth's voice, and the Bishop smiled in spite of himself. Here was a young man born to be a leader.

"Very well," he said. "I'll put it in the letter. But

tell me—do you really think the good friar can
spare us any workers for Poland?"

Ceslaus nodded eagerly. "Oh, yes, Uncle Ivo. I'm
quite sure he can. Why, just yesterday I heard it
said that in France alone Father Dominic has converted hundreds from heresy. Surely all this
couldn't have been done without many helpers?"

There was logic in these words, and the Bishop
completed his letter to Father Dominic in a happy
frame of mind. But an hour or so later, when he
retired for the night, it was not to sleep. Tired
though he was, he could not seem to relax. Again
and again he kept seeing the holy friar who had
presided that morning at the solemn inclosure of
the nuns at Saint Sixtus, who had offered Mass and
then raised a dead youth to life. Dominic de Guzman! What a remarkable man this was! And how
wonderful if he and his followers could come as
missionaries to Poland, even to Prussia and Lithuania and other pagan lands along the Baltic Sea.

"Our Northland needs preachers so much," he
thought sadly. "We have priests, it is true—but how
many are truly holy, truly wise? Oh, dear Lord,
please send us many of these white-clad friars,
these well-trained sons of the Spanish saint!"

Alas for the Bishop's hopes that the newly
founded Friars Preachers could come to Poland!
Ceslaus had spoken of them with more zeal than
knowledge, and when the little group of north-
erners arrived at the Monastery of Santa Sabina for
their interview with Dominic, an explanation was
in order.

"Your Lordship, I have only a very few sons," said Dominic gently. "Some are in Spain, others in France—a mere handful here in Italy. So you see it would be quite impossible to send even one friar to your country just now."

The Bishop's face fell. "We do need priests so much," he faltered, "especially in the cities. I was hoping, and my nephews were hoping...but of course we understand, Father Dominic. You have work to do here in the South. Our wish is that God may bless your labors a hundredfold."

To this Hyacinth and Ceslaus added a fervent "Amen," and for a moment all was quiet in the room. Then Dominic approached the two brothers, looking long and earnestly into their eyes.

"Perhaps all is not lost," he said kindly. "Your Lordship, why not give me some of these young men who have accompanied you here to Rome? In just a little while I would return them to you as true apostles."

The Bishop stared. Hyacinth, a friar? Ceslaus? But before he could form a reply, Hyacinth was on his knees. His hands were clasped, his face shining. "Do you mean it, Father Dominic? You would really have me in your Order?"

"Yes, my son. And in due course you would return to your north country. You would preach God's Truth there and convert many."

"You will have me as your son, too, Father?" whispered Ceslaus anxiously. "I am older than Hyacinth, yet without his learning. Still, I give you my word that I would do my best to follow instructions;

that not a day would pass..."

Dominic looked at the Bishop. "I think this young man speaks too humbly of himself, Your Lordship. Perhaps you would tell me the truth about him?"

Now Ivo Odrowatz, who had come to Rome for one purpose only: to be confirmed in his new post as Bishop of Cracow, was somewhat stunned at the sudden turn of events. Could it be that these nephews whom he had trained and encouraged for years in God's service were being rather too hasty in their decision to follow the Spanish friar?

"Ceslaus has degrees in theology and law from the University of Bologna," he said slowly. "He's been a priest at the Cathedral in Cracow for about five years..."

"And this younger brother? What of him?"

The Bishop gazed fondly at Hyacinth. "He, too, has a good education, Father Dominic. First at the University of Prague, then at Bologna. Like Ceslaus, he is now a canon of the Cathedral in Cracow. But do you really think...?"

Dominic smiled—understandingly, affectionately. "Do I really think that men who are already priests can take to living as simple friars without a struggle? Oh, Your Lordship, have no fear! You have asked for workers, for apostles in the North. Soon you will have them. And not only in Hyacinth and Ceslaus. There are others in your retinue whom God intends for His service."

The Bishop stared. "*Others*, Father Dominic?"

"Yes. I see one now—standing by the window.

"YOU WILL HAVE ME IN YOUR ORDER,
FATHER DOMINIC?"

And a second, by the door. Come here, my sons.
Tell me if it is not true that God has suddenly
touched your hearts with His grace—that now you
are both convinced you must give yourselves to
Him completely."

All eyes turned to where Dominic pointed, and
the Bishop gasped. Advancing toward the Spanish
friar were two of his lay attendants—Herman, who
hailed from Germany, and a young Czech named
Henry. They were good souls, honest and hard-
working, but never had the Bishop suspected that
they might be interested in the religious life.
Indeed, until this very moment they had seemed
quite content to spend their days as servants in the
episcopal household.

Dominic was smiling. "Well, Herman? Well,
Henry? What do you ask?"

With one accord the two fell upon their knees.
Yes, they also wished to be clothed in the habit of
the Friars Preachers. Of course they were not
priests like Ceslaus and Hyacinth. They had little
book learning. But they would do their best to be
of use in other ways if Father Dominic could find
room for them in his religious family.

The friar nodded understandingly. "Room, my
children? There is always room in a good work for
men who are willing to start in the lowest place."

Suddenly a lay Brother appeared in the doorway.
There was an approving smile on Dominic's face as
he observed that the newcomer had with him a
number of white woolen habits. Quickly turning to
the four young men before him, he indicated that

they should prostrate themselves on the ground in token of their unworthiness to serve God as religious. Then, as a second lay Brother approached with a lighted candle and Holy Water, he began to pray in a clear and fervent voice:

"Stretch forth, O Lord, unto these Thy servants, the right hand of Thy heavenly assistance, that they may seek Thee with all their hearts, and obtain what they fittingly ask..."

Bishop Ivo watched the little scene with a fast-beating heart. What an amazing day this was! He had come to beg for missionaries from Father Dominic de Guzman. Instead, the holy man had claimed both nephews and servants for his preaching Order. Yet even as he thought on this, reassuring words echoed in Ivo's ears:

"Why not give me some of these young men who have accompanied you here to Rome? In just a little while I would return them to you as true apostles."

Apostles! Apostles for Poland! God willing, the holy friar was right, thought the Bishop. Ceslaus and Hyacinth, even Herman and Henry, would do great things in the cause of Christ...

CHAPTER 2

A NEW LIFE

SOON THE four novices were settled in the Monastery of Santa Sabina, which had been given to Dominic by Pope Honorius the Third. They were supremely happy.

"It's as though I were a child again!" Hyacinth exclaimed one morning. "Oh, Father Dominic! How wonderful that I have given myself completely into your hands!"

Dominic shook his head. "Into God's hands," he corrected gently. "For see, my brother, no one in this monastery has given up his possessions, his freedom to come and go and do, just to please me. Rather, each has done these things to please the Heavenly Father. Each has done these things so that he may be a worthier instrument of the Divine Will."

Ceslaus looked up hopefully. "And surely this Will is that we return someday to Poland, Father Dominic? That we be missionaries to our own countrymen?"

The holy friar smiled. "Perhaps you may do even

10

more than that," he said slowly. "Perhaps you may
see many other lands than Poland, my son. But
whatever you do, wherever you go, there will be
many lessons to learn first. What do you say? Are
you willing to begin?"

The young priest replied eagerly. "Oh, yes,
Father Dominic! Please tell us everything we ought
to know."

So each day the four novices were instructed in
the ways and customs of the Order of Friars
Preachers. They discovered that one of the needs
which had prompted Dominic to begin his religious
family had been that of rooting out the Albigensian
heresy in France. This had been some five years
ago, in 1215, although actually a start had been
made before this date.

"In 1206, by the grace of God, I opened a convent at Prouille, in France," he said. "Nine noble
ladies, all converts from heresy, agreed to give
themselves to lives of prayer and sacrifice, so that
the work of our preaching friars might win favor
in God's eyes. And that is something which I would
have each of you remember, my brothers: men may
preach and write and study, even winning fame as
they gain souls for God, but all the while the grace
to do these things is not achieved by their own
merits. Rather does it come to them in great part
from the prayer and suffering of unknown souls."

Prayer and suffering! Soon Hyacinth and his companions had an even better understanding of these
spiritual weapons and of the reason for Dominic's
great success in winning souls for Christ. For

though he tried to keep his penances secret, the
novices more than once saw him in the middle of
the night, praying before the Tabernacle and offering to God the sacrifice of his sleep. Again, they
discovered that he fasted almost continually, and
wore about his waist a heavy iron chain.

"Our sisters in Prouille live under the Rule he
wrote for them," said Hyacinth. "They pray and suffer so that our sermons may touch many hearts. But
surely they have a constant companion in such
work. Father Dominic has given himself wholly to
God, and no suffering is too great for him if it
means winning a soul. Oh, my brothers! Let us ask
for grace to imitate such a good Father!"

So the four novices prayed very earnestly for the
gift of fortitude. They asked that they might bear
patiently all the sufferings sent them by Divine
Providence; also, that they might learn to make of
themselves really worthwhile instruments of the
Divine Will. Of course this would probably mean
added sufferings, such as their Father Dominic
inflicted upon himself. But to save even one soul
from Hell is worth any sacrifice.

"If we ask Him, God will give us such a love for
souls that we'll forget all about the suffering," said
Hyacinth confidently. "I'm sure this is one prayer
He always hears. What a pity that so few people
ever think of making it!"

So the days passed. Each morning saw the
novices assisting at the Holy Sacrifice of the Mass,
offered first by Dominic, later by one of the other
priests of the community. Then at stated intervals

they assembled in the chapel to chant the Divine Office. There was also considerable time devoted to solitary reading and study.

"Do you know why?" asked Father Tancred, the Prior of Santa Sabina, as the four walked with him one day in the monastery garden.

Ceslaus thought he knew. "Father Dominic wishes us to be well-informed when we go out against the heretics," he said quickly. "After all, our motto is *Veritas*—Truth. And a man has to read and study in order to answer false arguments. Isn't that so, Father Prior?"

The Prior nodded. "Yes—and we have another motto. *Contemplare, et contemplata aliis tradere.* What does that mean, Brother Henry?"

Remembering that he had been but a servant before his entrance into the Order, the young Czech hesitated at translating a Latin sentence in the presence of Fathers Hyacinth and Ceslaus. But out of obedience he rendered it, slowly: "To contemplate. . .and to give to others. . .the fruit of one's contemplation."

The Prior smiled at the strained look on the young man's face. "Correct. But put this thought in your own words, Brother. Tell us what it means to contemplate."

Once again Henry was a bit taken aback, and once again he did his best to obey. "Each morning I kneel down in my cell and empty my mind of all that is troubling me, Father Prior. I close my eyes. Then I look into myself. I try to understand that God dwells within my heart, since I have done my

"TELL US WHAT IT MEANS
TO CONTEMPLATE, BROTHER."

best to remain in the state of grace."

"Yes? What then?"

"Well, sometimes I just say 'Thank You' to Him for being there. At other times I say other things."

"For instance?"

Henry lowered his eyes. "I adore Him for being so good, so perfect. Then I thank Him for having made me and given me the chance to be happy with Him someday in Heaven."

Father Tancred was pleased. There was no doubt about it. Brother Henry had an excellent knowledge of contemplation. When he had completed his novitiate at Santa Sabina, he would give to others the fruits of this very simple but satisfactory thinking about God. Then he would be a true Friar Preacher.

Alas! Brother Henry might be at peace with himself and able to speak inspiringly about contemplation, but it was a different state of affairs with his friend and former co-worker in the Bishop's house, Brother Herman. As the days passed the youthful German was often overcome with a feeling of helplessness, of utter failure.

"I'm so stupid!" he moaned. "No matter how hard I try, I can't speak out well like the others. Oh, what am I going to do? How can I ever be a good preaching friar?"

There was a real problem here. Brother Herman had a willing spirit, but his brain did not take readily to study or reading. It was far easier for him to lift a hundred-pound weight in one hand than to spend fifteen minutes pondering the Holy Scriptures.

"Father Dominic, why did you ever take me into your family?" he mourned one day. "I'll never be of any use to you—even if I live to be a hundred years old!"

Dominic smiled. "Why not ask your Mother to help you?" he suggested. "Come—the two of us will go out into the garden and see what she can do."

"But surely my mother isn't in the garden, Father Dominic! Or any other place in Rome! She lives in Germany. Besides, even she always admitted that I would never make a scholar."

Dominic appeared not to have heard, and with one hand on his disciple's arm led him toward the open door. "Look," he said, pointing into the sunny garden. "What do you see, my son?"

Puzzled, Herman peered dutifully about. But after a few minutes he turned helplessly to his superior. Surely all was as usual? Shrubs, vines, flowers, yes—and many trees, including the orange tree planted some weeks before by Dominic himself. There was also the little fountain in the center of the garden, where now a number of small brown birds were splashing gaily. But certainly there was no sign of his mother. And why should there be? After all, this place of peace and quiet was in the cloistered part of the house. No woman could enter here.

"I don't see anything unusual," he confessed lamely. "Were you having a little fun with me, Father Dominic?"

Dominic laughed kindly. Poor Herman! He was

a slow-witted youth indeed. "No, my son. I just came to bring you to your Mother. See? There she is—over in the corner by the olive trees. Go to her, now, and ask her to help you in your troubles. Tell her everything. Remember, her power in Heaven and on earth is greater than that of any other creature."

Still puzzled, Herman looked to where his superior pointed. Then suddenly the light broke. Why, it was the Heavenly Mother of whom Dominic was speaking! Her shrine was over in the corner by the olive trees.

Like a child released from school, Herman ran happily across the garden and fell upon his knees before the little statue in its framework of vines and flowers. The doubts and fears were gone now. He understood perfectly what Father Dominic meant.

"Dearest Mother, please help me!" he whispered. "I'm very dull, you know—not at all good at books or at speaking in public. Oh, Seat of Wisdom, you who have so much power in Heaven, please give me the gift to win many souls for your Son! Please make me into a really useful friar. . .so that Father Dominic need never regret that he took me into his family!"

Soon an unaccustomed peace was creeping into Herman's soul. After a moment he began to recite the familiar *Pater* and *Ave*. He might be slow at books, but he knew one thing at least: it was a matter of ordinary courtesy to pay the Blessed Mother some little mark of respect if he wished her to hear his request.

"I'll come every day, with Father Dominic's permission, and pray before this little shrine," he thought. "Dearest Mother, does that please you?"

The statue in its rustic setting did not suddenly come to life. There was no blinding vision, no sound of heavenly voices; but deep in his heart Herman felt that all was well. The Blessed Mother *was* pleased. She would come to his aid.

Dominic would much have preferred to remain in the garden, joining his prayer to that of his young disciple, but suddenly a lay Brother came hurrying down the corridor. Could Father Dominic come at once? His Lordship, the Bishop of Cracow, had just arrived on a matter of vital importance.

The holy friar smiled, understanding only too well the reason for the episcopal visit. For some weeks good Bishop Ivo had been growing impatient to return to the North. His business in the Eternal City had been settled long ago. It was time to be thinking of Poland. If at all possible, he wished to return to his native land accompanied by Hyacinth, Ceslaus, Henry and Herman.

"I know three months isn't a very long time for training as a friar," said the Bishop apologetically. "But I do have to go home, Father Dominic. And I'm selfish enough to want to do so with my four young friends. Don't you think it could be arranged?"

Dominic hesitated. Humanly speaking, a novitiate of only three months was far too short. Ordinarily, Hyacinth and his companions should spend at least a year in prayer and study before being allowed to consecrate themselves to God by vow. After that, if all went well, they could do a little preaching in and around the Holy City, while still following the community life at Santa Sabina. But to be taken away from their training so soon? And to a strange and pagan land?

Dominic looked closely at the Bishop. "I believe that conditions are not too good for the Church in Poland, Your Lordship, and that you really do need preaching friars."

Ivo nodded, his face a study in deep dejection. Poland, as was the case with all other northern countries, was an ignorant land. Even the clergy were affected. The sooner holy men from the outside could take up work there, the better for all concerned.

CHAPTER 3

NORTHWARD THE COURSE

THAT SAME day Dominic reached a decision. In a week's time Bishop Ivo's young friends would complete their novitiate and start for Cracow, in Poland. He himself would accompany them on the first stages of the journey, as already Pope Honorius and his court had left Rome for Viterbo and Dominic had been ordered to follow as special preacher to His Holiness. There was also urgent business in Bologna, where the first General Chapter of the Order was scheduled to be held on the Feast of Pentecost.

The little group set out for the North one sunny morning in early May. As befitted his position as Bishop of Cracow, Ivo rode in a special coach. Before and behind him went his several attendants, each mounted on a horse. The friars were on foot, however, since their Rule prescribed that they should always travel in the simplest manner possible. After all, were they not members of a mendicant Order—that is, a religious family which owned no property of its own, whose priests and Brothers

HOW GOOD TO BE ABOUT THE
LORD'S WORK AT LAST!

even went from door to door begging their bread from the faithful?

The four young men in their white habits and black cloaks, staffs in their hands and packs upon their backs, were in exceedingly high spirits. How good to be about the Lord's work at last! And oh, to have wings on one's feet, so that one might reach the pagan Northland very quickly!

"How long do you think it will take us to walk to Poland?" asked Henry eagerly. "Three months or four?"

Ceslaus laughed. "Two months will be plenty, for surely the distance from Rome to Cracow is no more than seven hundred and fifty miles. Since we're young and healthy. . ."

"My brothers, we can reach Cracow in fifty days if we walk fifteen miles a day," said another voice suddenly. "But I do not think we should journey that quickly. There will be many places where the people will want us to stay a while and preach."

Ceslaus looked up in amazement. Could this be Brother Herman who spoke so confidently? who worked a little problem in numbers as quickly as any man?

Seeing the surprised expressions on every face, Herman turned a deep and fiery red. Oh, that he had kept silence! Certainly this was not the time or place to tell his companions that of late he was finding it a little easier to read and to figure. Of course Father Dominic knew the secret: how he prayed every day to Our Lady, Seat of Wisdom, that she would enlighten his mind and make him into a worthy friar. But as for the others...

"I...I was just thinking out loud," he mumbled apologetically. "I didn't mean to interrupt you, Father Ceslaus. Please go on."

Dominic smiled as he took note of the little scene. But deep in his heart there was a genuine sadness. Well he knew that the approaching farewell with these beloved sons would be a lasting one. In a year or so his earthly labors would be over. His little family would have to find another leader after August 6, 1221.

"I'll be fifty-one years old when the call comes," he thought. "Oh, Heavenly Father, please grant me the grace to live completely united to Your Will until the end! How well I know that only in this way can I be really pleasing to You!"

The hours passed, and the May sun mounted higher in the heavens. By now Rome had been left far behind and the friars were beginning to show signs of the many dusty miles they had traveled. Suddenly Dominic realized that his young companions had fallen silent, that they had slowed their steps and now were looking at him anxiously.

"You're quite pale, Father," said Hyacinth contritely. "I'm afraid we've been walking too fast for you."

"Yes, how thoughtless of us!" put in Henry. "Look, Father, there's a big oak tree over on that hill. Wouldn't you like to rest a while in the shade?"

Dominic shook his head, assuring his young disciples that he was feeling perfectly well. However, Brother Herman's reminder that soon it would be time to recite the Divine Office was received with universal relief. Now all could stop with a clear conscience in the shade of the big oak.

So it was done, and for some thirty minutes the quiet countryside echoed to the melodious chant of the Psalms.

"Incline Thine ear, O Lord, and hear me; for I am needy and poor," declared Brothers Henry and Herman.

"Preserve my soul, for I am holy; save Thy servant, O my God, that trusteth in Thee," replied the others.

"Have mercy on me, O Lord, for I have cried to Thee all the day."

"Give joy to the soul of Thy servant, for to Thee, O Lord, I have lifted up my soul."

So the friars prayed, not in words of their own choosing but in the official words of the Church. This was the liturgy, or divine service, which they had promised to perform every day of their lives. In these psalms they would adore the God who had created them out of nothing; they would thank Him for the many graces He had given them; they would beg pardon for having offended Him by sin; they would ask His blessing on themselves and on their work.

Of course the Holy Sacrifice of the Mass was the day's greatest prayer, whether for priest or layman, but the Divine Office was also very important. It provided a setting for the Mass—beginning very early in the morning with the offering of Matins and Lauds, then ending at night with the beautiful prayer of Compline. Only the most serious reasons could excuse a friar from participating in this continual liturgy, or worship of God.

When their prayers were finished, Hyacinth undertook a pious deception. Would Father Dominic give a short talk before they went farther on their journey? Not a sermon—just a few words on the Christian life.

The latter's eyes twinkled. He was not in the least deceived as to the reason for the suggestion. Plainly it was this: Hyacinth feared that additional walking in the noonday sun would be too much for Father Dominic's fifty years. Therefore, anything which furnished an excuse for resting was much to be desired. And of course in one way he was right. Yet the founder of the Friars Preachers was not prepared to let the ruse pass unchallenged.

"Why don't *you* give the little talk?" he countered pointedly. "Tell me again about Poland, my son. That way I can listen and really take things easy."

Hyacinth looked closely at his beloved superior, then shrugged his shoulders in a cheerful admission of defeat. He might have known it. Father Dominic was too clever a man to be fooled by anyone or anything. He had one of the best minds in Europe—such a mind, indeed, that three years before, Pope Honorius had made him Master of the Sacred Palace—that is, his own special adviser, preacher and theologian at the Vatican.

"I'll be glad to tell you about Poland, Father," he replied eagerly. "Shall I start from the beginning?"

Dominic nodded. "Yes, with the year 965. If I remember correctly, it was then that the Christian religion made its entrance into your country."

So Hyacinth arose and faced his brethren, who remained seated on the grass under the giant oak. A thrill of pride ran through the Spanish friar as he settled himself to listen, for Hyacinth was an imposing figure. The white habit and black cloak of the Order lent his stalwart frame a certain grace, and the sunlight which filtered through the branches of the great oak cast its own spell upon him—playing up the flaxen hair, the blue eyes that flashed with zeal or grew dark with sorrow as the young Pole spoke of conditions in his native land.

"Not much is known of our country before the tenth century," he began. "Since only a part faces on the sea—and the northerly Baltic Sea at that—there was never any trade with the civilized world to the south. Both Italy and Greece heard the message of Christianity very early, from the Apostles and Disciples, but Poland was left in darkness for centuries. As a result, the people remained rough, cruel and ignorant. There was constant warfare between the tribes."

"Tell us about Prince Mieszko," put in Ceslaus suddenly. "That's where the story really begins."

Hyacinth agreed. "Prince Mieszko was the first Polish ruler whose name has come down to us, although there were at least three others before him. All seem to have had trouble with the Germans, their neighbors to the west, who were determined to push their boundaries into Polish territory. The Poles were just as determined that they should not. After being twice defeated by an arrogant German count, Mieszko had an idea. To protect himself from further trouble with Germany, he would seek an alliance with Bohemia, a Christian country to the south. He would do this by marrying a Bohemian princess named Dubravka."

To Ceslaus, this story of Poland's early days was thoroughly familiar, yet it never lost interest. He listened as attentively as the others to Hyacinth's clear explanation.

"Mieszko was a pagan, but when he married Dubravka in 965 he agreed to adopt her Christian faith. Actually he did not have very much interest in religion. His principal desire was to secure an ally in the constant struggles with Germany. However, after his Baptism he set no limits to missionary activities in Poland. Soon the whole country was adopting the new faith, and monasteries began to arise in various parts. Most of these were Cistercian monasteries—that is, the monks living there were followers of the Rule of Saint Benedict in its strict form."

The minutes slipped by, and still Hyacinth spoke on. He described the fine results achieved by the Cistercians as they labored in remote swamps and forests, clearing the land, teaching new methods of agriculture to the Poles, teaching them also the message of Christian living. Then there was the fact that shortly after his conversion, Prince Mieszko had placed all of Poland under the protection of the Pope. Henceforth the country was considered as belonging to the civilized western world, as opposed to Russia and other territories in the East. It could not be invaded by anyone, for any purpose whatsoever, without incurring the disapproval of the Holy See.

"Prince Mieszko died in 992," continued Hyacinth. "His eldest son, Boleslaus the First, also called the Brave, strengthened and extended the country's influence, and it was during his reign that Poland was given her first native Archbishop—in the city of Gniezno. Now it was no longer necessary for the German Archbishop of Magdeburg to watch over the spiritual interests of the Poles. Pagans until just a few years before, they had rapidly assumed a surprising independence and wished to govern themselves in spiritual as well as temporal matters."

Soon Hyacinth had left behind the comparatively successful career of Boleslaus the First (which lasted until 1025) and was launching into the trials and troubles that befell his descendants. He minced no words. Poland, although it had accepted the Catholic Faith in the days of Prince Mieszko, had never been a peaceful country. And this was largely due to one fact: namely, that the eldest son of a noble house did not automatically succeed to his father's lands and power. Rather, these were divided among all the sons—and generally there were bitterness and argument as to whether or not the division was a just one.

"There have been feuds and battles without number in such cases," said Hyacinth sadly. "Brother kills brother and seizes his lands, so that he may be more powerful. Soon he meets a man who has done just the same thing. They fight each other, taxing the people to provide for their armies. Then thousands upon thousands of young men are killed. Many sins are committed, homes are destroyed, and there is no time to think about God, to provide training and education for the poor. Oh, my friends! Don't you see why apostles must hurry to the North? The nobles there must be taught to see Christ in other human beings! The peasants, fighting and dying in a foolish cause, must be taught the same!"

Dominic's eyes shone. What an immense field for good lay in northern Europe! And how fine if he could go there with these zealous young disciples! It would be as fruitful a trip as the one he had longed to make to Asia in his early manhood. But even as he thought on this, a shadow crossed his face. Sixteen years ago, by express command of Pope Innocent the Third, Asia had been denied him as a missionary field. He had been forced to set aside the glorious thought of dying as a martyr at the hands of the barbarian Tartars living there and to concentrate instead on rooting out the Albigensian heresy in southern France. Now it would seem that, with the same spirit of abandonment to God's Will, he must set aside the thought of going to Poland. What strength he had should be spent in training others to be missionaries, not wasted in foolish day-dreams.

"But my spirit will go forth with Hyacinth and his friends," he thought. "God will grant this one

CHAPTER 4

THE FATHER

FROM TIME to time Ivo's carriage stopped, so that Dominic and his friars might catch up with the Bishop's party. Then there was always much joyful talk and planning, for Bishop Ivo could hardly wait to reach Cracow. What a wonderful welcome would be accorded there to his four young friends!

"No one in the city has even seen a friar before," he said. "Oh, Father Dominic! Think what it will be like that day when your sons preach in the Cathedral for the first time!"

Dominic smiled. His imagination was supplying him with a vivid picture of what it would be like. Cracow's largest church would not be big enough to hold the vast crowd. Then Hyacinth and the others would have to preach in the streets, with the usual results: young men who had never given a thought to becoming religious would be impelled by the grace of God to ask for admission into the new preaching Order. Very soon there would be a monastery of Friars Preachers in the city—a monastery filled with fervent novices and postulants.

Soon, however, there were no more cheerful plans and conversations by the roadside. The travelers had reached Viterbo, and it was time for Dominic to say farewell to the Bishop and to his beloved sons.

On that morning when all assembled for the last time, there were tears in every eye. However, none felt the approaching separation more keenly than Hyacinth. Suddenly he was overwhelmed with discouragement at the thought of what awaited him in Poland. How foolish he had been to think that he and his companions could accomplish a complete conversion of the country! Of course he himself was a priest, and likewise his brother Ceslaus, with years of study behind them. Still, neither had had more than a few months' training in the religious life. They should be now but simple novices back at Santa Sabina—taking orders from their superiors, learning to unite their wills to the Will of God.

"Father Dominic, we can't go on without you!" he cried, suddenly dismayed. "We know too little!"

Until this point Ceslaus and the others had held their true feelings in check. Now, finding that Hyacinth had confessed his weakness and doubts, they crowded around their beloved leader with their own various fears. "Don't leave us, Father!" they begged. "We'll never be able to do anything without you!"

Dominic looked at the four anxious faces before him, and his heart ached. Never again, at least in this world, would he see these beloved disciples. Yet now that the moment of parting had come, he must not show that his sorrow was equal to, if not even greater than, theirs. The Devil was waiting for just such a display of weakness so that he might figure out a clever temptation.

"Look, my sons," he said cheerfully. "We are now many miles from Santa Sabina, our convent in Rome. And we have left the Prior, Father Tancred, in charge there. Isn't that so?"

Since Dominic's eyes were upon him especially, Brother Henry nodded in agreement. "Yes, Father. That's right."

"Very well. Now, is there any way we can still help Father Prior in his work—as we rest here in Viterbo, or later when we continue our travels?"

Henry was on the point of shaking his head when a sudden light dawned in his eyes. "We can help him by prayer, Father, no matter where we are."

"Prayer? What kind of prayer would you suggest?"

Somehow the young Czech's spirits began to rise as he entered into the familiar game of question and answer with his beloved superior. "The Holy Sacrifice of the Mass is the greatest prayer of all. If we really want to help Father Prior, we ought to remember him at the altar each morning and ask God to bless him."

"An excellent idea, Brother Henry. And is that all we can do?"

"Well...we could also remember him in lesser prayers throughout the day."

"For instance?"

"Once in a while we could say the *Our Father.* Or perhaps the *Hail Mary.*"

"But these are just short prayers! Of what help would they be?"

Brother Henry was quite taken aback. "But it isn't the *length* of a prayer that counts, Father! It's the *way* it's said! I'm very sure that God hears any prayer which comes from the heart, no matter how short it is."

For a moment all was silent, so that the ringing echoes of Henry's voice lingered in every ear. Then slowly, quietly, came the peace and understanding which Dominic, by a special gift of the Holy Spirit, always instilled into his followers and which he had planned should result from this little game with Brother Henry. Now the brethren realized even better than before that God hears each honest prayer that comes from our heart. And they also understood that it would be in this same kind of prayer—made quietly before the Blessed Sacrament or with difficulty in the midst of a day's wearisome occupations—that they would help and also join with one another. Even death would not make any difference, for the prayers of the living and the dead are but so many roads leading to a single destination—God!

"Our bodies may be far apart, but our souls can always meet and be happy in Him," said Dominic softly. "Think about this, my sons, when your duties seem too overpowering, when you are lonely and discouraged and Heaven seems very far away. For Heaven, and those we love, are at no greater distance from us than can be spanned by a small and fervent prayer."

Presently all knelt for the blessing of their father and superior—heads bowed, hearts filled to overflowing. Then suddenly Bishop Ivo touched Hyacinth on the shoulder. Dominic was gone!

"It's time for us to go, too," he said. "My son, will you be ready to leave for Orvieto this afternoon?"

Hyacinth nodded. Orvieto, Siena, Florence, Bologna, Venice—there was a long way to travel before they reached the north of Italy and the road that would take them over the mountains to their native Poland.

"Yes, Uncle Ivo," he said gently. "We'll be ready. You go before us and we'll follow at our regular pace."

Even as he spoke, Hyacinth managed a slight smile. Perhaps he ought to remember these words, for they were his first as superior of the little group. Yes—just before the final blessing, Dominic had placed him in charge of Ceslaus, Henry and Herman. Henceforth these three owed him complete obedience, for he had taken Dominic's place and was now their father.

"May God help me in this new work!" he thought. "It isn't going to be easy to have so much responsibility."

The four young friars trudged steadily northward. Following Dominic's example, they tried to spend each night at some monastery, so that there would be an opportunity to offer the Holy Sacrifice the next morning—also to join in prayer in the peaceful atmosphere of a house consecrated to God. On their travels they occasionally met other friars—not clad like themselves, however, in habits of white wool with black cloaks about their shoulders, but barefoot and in the rough brown garments of another Order—that of the Friars Minor, founded a few years previous by the holy Francis of Assisi.

"There is a deep understanding between Friar Francis and Father Dominic," Hyacinth told Bishop Ivo one day. "Although Francis isn't a priest, Father Dominic considers him a really learned man. He said once that it was Friar Francis who taught him the true meaning of Holy Poverty."

Ivo nodded. "Someday I hope to meet the good Friar Francis," he said. "How old a man would he be, I wonder?"

Hyacinth did a little figuring. "Our Father Dominic is fifty years old, Uncle. I believe Friar Francis is quite a bit younger—about thirty-eight."

The young superior thoroughly enjoyed this and other little chats with his uncle. Indeed, Ceslaus and he considered the Bishop their second father and reverenced him accordingly. Well they knew that if Poland and other countries in the North could have spiritual leaders such as Ivo, conditions would be immeasurably improved in both Church and State. For a zealous and holy priest has an enormous influence over others. It is next to impossible for the souls under his care to go astray. Of course they may drift for a while, may even deliberately set themselves up against the one who would save them. But in the end, through prayer and sacrifice,

THEY TRIED TO SPEND EACH NIGHT
AT SOME MONASTERY.

the good pastor will win. He will reclaim each lost sheep and bring it back to the Fold.

"Lord, give me the grace to be a truly holy priest," Hyacinth often prayed. "Let me have some of Uncle Ivo's wonderful spirit. Let me give it to others, so that Poland may profit and become a land of souls who believe in You, who will suffer and die a thousand deaths rather than betray Your cause."

More and more the thought persisted in the young superior's mind that perhaps it was just as well that there were only four of them to go as missionaries to Cracow. Since they were so few, and with but three months' training as religious, they would have to be humble. And being humble, it would be easier to be holy. Only proud men find it hard to give themselves completely into the hands of God. Only proud men, and those who are afraid of His Most Holy Will.

"And much of the time such pride and fear are related," Hyacinth told himself. "The Devil uses both most skillfully to keep souls from realizing that they are meant to be *children,* and children of a *kindly* Father; that this is the way most people are called to be saints. Ah, perhaps I should give this thought to the others. It might help them when the time comes to preach to our countrymen."

The time to preach! As Herman had foretold at the outset of the trip, this came long before the four friars had reached Poland. In fact, once they had left Italy and crossed into the province of Carinthia, in southern Austria, they found themselves besieged by curious crowds.

"What did I tell you?" cried Bishop Ivo excitedly. "The whole of Europe is eager for Father Dominic's preachers. Can you guess what message just arrived from the Archbishop of Salzburg?"

Hyacinth looked up quickly. Surely the Archbishop hadn't invited the little group to come to his own city! If so, it would be impossible to accept, for this would delay the arrival in Poland by several weeks.

"Ah, there's not only an invitation to Salzburg," said Ivo, reading his nephew's thoughts, "but the Archbishop says he is going to take us there in person. The message states that he will wait for us in Friesach—the mining center that lies ahead in the mountains."

This was truly disturbing news, and there was much serious discussion as to what ought to be done. Naturally the final decision would have to rest with Hyacinth, since he was the superior, but Bishop Ivo counseled him not to be too hasty. The Archbishop of Salzburg was extremely fond of Father Dominic. The two had met years ago in Rome, and it was to be expected that the prelate would want to hear the latest news of his old friend.

"At least we can go to Friesach and tell him Father Dominic is traveling in northern Italy these days," he said. "And we can also explain about the need for reaching Poland quickly. After all, the Archbishop is a reasonable man, my son. He won't urge you to work in his city if it's really impossible."

Hyacinth smiled. He had just been confronted with his first real problem as superior of the three other friars. Of course it was not a very large problem, but for a while it had disturbed his carefully laid plans and hence his peace of mind. And this was wrong. It was not the way for the father of a family to act.

"Uncle Ivo," he said suddenly, "let's kneel down."

Once again Hyacinth was about to prove his humility—and his wisdom. He was going to put himself and his little company completely at God's disposal. He was going to offer the prayer of utter abandonment to His Most Holy Will. Very soon the answer to the present problem would come, and with it a peace and happiness beyond all understanding.

CHAPTER 5

FIRST FRUITS

WHEN THE friars reached Friesach, the whole city turned out to greet them. Never before had the people seen religious whose vocation it was to travel from one town to another, preaching the Word of God. Heretofore they had known only two types of clergy: the cloistered sons of Saint Benedict, whose monasteries lay far out in the country, and the canons of the Cathedral, who dispensed the Sacraments and recited the Divine Office at stated intervals throughout the day. But that there should also be men who gave themselves to God's service and still remained in the world, going daily among the people, preaching and instructing as did the newly arrived friars from Rome, was something new. It was so new, in fact, that it fascinated several young men in Friesach. Before many days had passed, a number had applied for admission into the Order.

The Archbishop of Salzburg could not help smiling as he greeted Hyacinth one July afternoon. The latter's face was so solemn!

"Well, my son, don't you like it here in
Friesach?" he asked kindly. "Haven't we been able
to make you feel at home these past six weeks?"

Hyacinth gave a deep sigh. "Your Excellency, you
and all the others have been most kind. But. . .well,
I've just had an interview with another good soul
who says he wants to be a friar."

"Splendid! And how many does that make?"

"Fifty, Your Excellency. But that's not the point."

"No?"

"No. You see, this particular young man comes
from a very wealthy family. Perhaps you know to
whom I refer?"

Once again amusement flickered briefly in the
Archbishop's eyes. "You mean Helger, son of the
Count of Hochstein?"

"Yes, Your Excellency."

"But he's a good lad! And so is his friend Ulric.
Indeed, Ulric has been blessed by God in no ordinary way. When he prays, wonderful things happen.
Make no mistake about it, my son. You'll never
regret taking these two into the Order."

Hyacinth sighed once more. "I'm not worried
about Helger or Ulric, Your Excellency. But when
I think of *fifty* young men. . .and dukes and counts
among them. . .oh, it does seem as though there
will have to be a delay in our leaving Friesach!
Since God has sent these children, surely He
means that they should be looked after—at least for
a while?"

The Archbishop nodded slowly. But as he sought
to console the young friar over the sudden setback

to his plans, he found that Hyacinth was not too disappointed. Indeed, in the depths of his soul he was at peace. Every day he united himself and his little company to the Divine Will. And this action, inspired by the Holy Spirit, always produced a wonderful happiness, even in the midst of external trials. It seemed that God was pleased with such a display of faith and love. Because Hyacinth had given himself completely into His hands, He flooded his soul with the choicest of graces.

"Maybe you'll tell me how long I ought to stay here in Friesach?" asked the young superior suddenly. "Also, what is to be done with the fifty novices?"

The Archbishop looked out of the window. A huge crowd had gathered in the public square, and every face was turned in the direction of the church steps. Apparently one of Hyacinth's little band was preaching, and the prelate noted thankfully that the audience was hanging on every word. Ah, how good God was, he reflected, to have sent such true apostles to Austria—men who were literally remaking the city of Friesach! For these daily sermons in the public square were only part of the work undertaken by the friars since their arrival six weeks ago. Always, after the sermons, there were long lines of men and women waiting to go to Confession. Throughout the city the secular clergy were busier than they had ever been before. And because of the increased reception of the Sacraments, vice had almost disappeared in Friesach. There was much more happiness in family and in individual life.

"WHAT IS TO BE DONE WITH THE FIFTY NOVICES,
YOUR EXCELLENCY?"

"If you want my true opinion, Father Hyacinth," said the Archbishop thoughtfully, "it's this: stay with us until October. By that time arrangements will have been made for the housing of the novices. You will appoint a Prior from among your followers. Then, the new convent having been dedicated. . ."

"Then I will come to Salzburg?"

The Archbishop shook his head. "Ah, that would be too much of a sacrifice, my son. No, in October you will go to Poland. God willing, you will start to labor among your own people at last."

The weeks passed, and the Archbishop put at Hyacinth's disposal a large building near the Cathedral. With a few alterations, it served as a monastery for the friars. Indeed, there was even a resemblance between it and the convent of Santa Sabina in Rome, and Hyacinth marveled at the wonderful ways of God. In a city which Dominic had never seen there was now a monastery of his sons, filled to capacity in just a few months' time! And its founder was a Polish priest who was not yet a religious of one year's standing!

"Perhaps Uncle Ivo will say that all this is worth the disappointment of having to go on to Cracow without us," Hyacinth told himself one morning. "Just think! Here in Friesach is the first monastery of German-speaking Friars Preachers in the whole world!"

Yes, it was a wonderful thought, and not a day passed that the entire community did not offer grateful prayers in the chapel. But even as he prayed, Hyacinth knew that soon he must come to grips with another problem. September was drawing to a close. In a few days he must leave Friesach for Cracow, where his uncle was awaiting him impatiently. And before he went, a Prior would have to be installed in the new monastery.

"And who will it be?" he often wondered, kneeling before the crucifix in his cell. "Dearest Lord, I know that someday I must sacrifice the companionship of my brother Ceslaus. But do You really wish that I leave him here in Friesach? Please tell me!"

The familiar little prayer was just finished one day when there came a knock at the door. Rising from his knees, Hyacinth went to open it and found that Brother Herman had come with a message. Two young men wished an interview with the superior. They were downstairs now, and by the looks of things they were University students, of good family and character, who wanted to become friars.

"Are you able to see them right away, Father, or shall I tell them to come back later?"

Hyacinth shook his head. "I'll see them in a moment. Just now, though, I'd like a word with you, Brother. Will you come in?"

Herman stepped into his superior's cell. It was a very small room and might have belonged to the humblest member of the community. A bed made of planks stood in one corner, while near the window was a large table with a chair on either side. There were no pictures on the rough plaster walls—only a crucifix and a Holy Water font. But there were several books, somewhat battered and worn, bearing witness to the fact that in this little room lived a true Friar Preacher—one who prayed and studied before going out to preach and govern others.

"Sit down, my son," said Hyacinth kindly. "And don't worry about the two young men downstairs. They'll be looked after soon."

As Herman took the chair his superior indicated, his heart rejoiced. It had been quite a while since there had been a chance to talk privately with Father Hyacinth. The recent days had been such busy ones for him, what with the many sermons in the public square, the opening of the new monastery, the reception and training of fifty novices. And at night things were not much different, for then Hyacinth gave himself to long and loving prayer before the Blessed Sacrament, realizing full well that a man never accomplishes anything of himself, not even the smallest task. All grace and strength come from God, and come in truly greater abundance if they are asked for frequently and humbly upon one's knees.

"Now you're having a really wise thought, Brother Herman," said Hyacinth as he seated himself at the other side of the table. "Prayer is certainly the most wonderful medicine in the world. And none of us ever grows strong enough to do without it."

As had happened so many times, Herman did not even notice this bit of mind-reading. He leaned forward with childlike eagerness.

"Prayer *is* wonderful, Father. Do you know that last week I made up a little one of my own and dedicated it to the Blessed Mother? Ever since then it has brought me great comfort."

"Really? And what is this prayer, Brother?"

"Sweetest Jesus, grant that I may praise with my mouth, cherish with my heart and honor by my actions Thy most loving Mother and mine."

For a moment Hyacinth was silent, gazing long and tenderly at the young religious. And as he gazed, he was struck with sudden joy. *Herman was a saint!* For months he had prayed faithfully to the Blessed Mother for help with his work. Since he was convinced that he was stupid, a good-for-nothing when it came to study and preaching, his prayers had been rooted in unusual humility. He had recognized his own nothingness, was even content to remain stupid if this were God's Will. Yet he had never stopped trying to improve. Always he had remembered that Father Dominic had clothed him with the habit of a Friar Preacher for some special reason, that he must do all in his power to be true to the wonderful gift of his vocation. Prayer was required of him, of course—humble and persevering—but work was required, too, and early in his religious life Herman had discovered the worth of these twin tools with which each man in the world must build his ladder to Heaven. He had discovered them and called upon the Blessed Mother for assistance in their use. And of course she had answered the prayer of a trusting child. Every day, slowly, surely, Herman was progressing in both the spiritual and the intellectual life.

Presently Hyacinth arose and placed a kindly hand upon his young follower's shoulder. "Brother, do you know that I had a real problem to solve when you came to see me just now? And that suddenly everything is settled?"

Herman restrained all questions. "I'm glad of that, Father. You have far too much to think about these days."

"Maybe. But do you know what this problem was?"

"No, Father. Unless it had something to do with the two young men who are waiting to see you downstairs. But then, you don't know who they are...and I forgot to ask their names..."

"Brother, the problem that has been bothering me is this: I must go to Cracow very soon. And before I go, I must appoint a superior to look after this first convent of our friars in Austria. I've thought about my own brother, but something tells me that Father Ceslaus is meant for other work. Now, do you know who would be a good Prior for this house in Friesach?"

Herman hesitated. Who was he to give an opinion on such a problem? Yet since it was Father Hyacinth who asked...

"Brother Henry is a good soul, Father. He's a Czech, but he speaks German fluently, and that would be useful here. Then he's well on his way to completing the studies for the priesthood..."

Hyacinth shook his head. "Our first Prior in Friesach will not be Brother Henry. He will be you, my son."

Herman stared, dumbfounded. *He,* the Prior? *He,* to have complete charge of the new monastery, including the training of fifty novices? Surely he had not heard Father Hyacinth correctly! Why, he was far from ready for the priesthood! And as for his preaching. . .

"Our Lady will help you in this new work," continued Hyacinth evenly. "Remember, she was but a fourteen-year-old girl when Gabriel came and announced that she was to be the Mother of God. And what did she reply?"

"Behold the handmaid of the Lord. Be it done unto me according to thy word," said Herman, slowly.

"That's right. Well, suppose you think about these words for the rest of the day, Brother. And don't worry because you are now the Prior of Friesach yet not a priest. Our Lady will continue to enlighten your mind, and study will become still easier for you. In due course you will be ordained and lead many to God."

Herman was standing like one in a dream. "Yes, Father. Thank you, Father. But. . .but what do I do now?"

There was a twinkle in Hyacinth's eyes as he took the new Prior by the arm and led him toward the door. "What about the two young men downstairs? Now that you are superior, they have come to discuss their vocations with you, not me. Go, my son, and see if God is calling them to be preaching friars."

Abruptly Herman fell upon his knees. "Please give me your blessing first!" he begged. "I. . .I feel so weak, Father!"

So Hyacinth raised his hand in priestly blessing, and with all the fervor at his command implored the Father, Son and Holy Ghost to assist the newly appointed Prior of Friesach. On the surface it would seem that Herman had only a slight chance for success, but long ago Hyacinth had learned to laugh at merely human standards. This was no time to be content with a minimum of faith. It was a moment that required complete submission to God's Will, complete assurance that grace would be forthcoming for the most difficult tasks, if only it was asked for in the spirit of a confident child.

"Go, my son," he said finally. "I place in your hands this monastery, the first fruits of our work in the North. May it yield you a truly splendid harvest!"

CHAPTER 6

A POOR MAN COMES TO CRACOW

THE SAME day that saw Herman's appointment as Prior also brought news from Andreas, the Bishop of Prague. He had heard that Dominic's friars were in Austria on their way to Poland, and with all the eloquence he could muster he pleaded that Hyacinth send him at least one preacher.

"You and your brother Ceslaus were University students here not so long ago," he said. "You know that our city does not have enough priests, that many souls are being lost every day for lack of Christian instruction. Oh, my son! In God's Name, send me one of your children! Prague is so hungry for Truth!"

Hyacinth looked long and thoughtfully at the Bishop's letter, then sent for Ceslaus. Somehow he felt that the time for separation had come.

"I think you had better take Brother Jerome and go to Prague," he said. "The Bishop has given us a house near the Church of Saint Clement. With God's help, you will fill it with novices just as we have done here."

Not even by the flicker of an eyelash did Ceslaus betray his true feelings, for long ago under Dominic's direction he had learned the value of obedience. Instead, he gave Hyacinth a cheerful smile and knelt for his blessing. But the younger brother understood that the new assignment must carry with it a certain disappointment. It meant that now Ceslaus might not see home and loved ones in Poland for a long time, since Prague was more than two hundred miles west of Cracow and there would be little time for anything but hard work once the city was reached.

Quietly he placed his hands on Ceslaus' head and prayed that comforting words would come to him, wondering for still another time why Father Dominic had made him, the younger brother, superior of the group that had set out from Rome more than five months ago. Yet, sensing his weakness, he sensed a certain strength, too.

"Ceslaus," he whispered suddenly, "do you remember how we used to wonder at Father Dominic's great success as a preacher?"

Ceslaus smiled. "Yes. But we soon discovered the reason. He paid the price for other people's sins. The fruitful sermons sprang from sacrifices—small and large."

"I know. And somehow it seems that it ought to be the same with us. If we really want to do great things for souls, shouldn't we disregard our own feelings? Shouldn't we be willing to do anything God asks, even if it means..."

"Even if it means never seeing each other again?"

Hyacinth looked long and earnestly into his brother's eyes. Ah, so Ceslaus did understand!

"That would be true suffering, wouldn't it?" he asked presently, "with power to purchase many souls from sin?"

Ceslaus did not answer right away. To be separated from this younger brother would be much more than suffering in the ordinary sense. It would be akin to a slow and excruciating death. Yet of course Hyacinth was right. Only by dying to earthly joys are men made ready for the joys of Heaven. Therefore. . .

"If we ask God to help us, we can make *any* sacrifice," he said finally. "So I will go to Prague, Hyacinth—or anywhere else you wish to send me—and go with a happy heart. And here and now perhaps I had better say good-bye. May Our Lady bless you always—and prosper your work, wherever it may be."

Scarcely knowing whence came the idea, Hyacinth suddenly felt convinced that countries other than Poland would profit from the labors of Ceslaus and himself. Between them, and with God's help, they would spread the True Faith over much of Europe. "You will go to Bohemia, Silesia and Germany," he said, not realizing that his voice had taken on strange and prophetic tones. "I will go to Poland, Ruthenia, Lithuania and Prussia. And every day we will meet in prayer at the altar, as Father Dominic taught us."

The farewell was not prolonged. Before many hours had passed, Ceslaus was on his way to

THE FAREWELL WAS NOT PROLONGED.

Prague, accompanied by Brother Jerome, a young man who had joined the Order at Friesach and who had been allowed to complete his novitiate much sooner than usual. Both friars were on foot for their journey of two hundred miles due north. And Hyacinth and Brother Henry, having bade farewell to Herman and his novices, were also on foot for their projected trip to Cracow—some three hundred and twenty-five miles to the northeast. And why? Because being vowed to poverty, it was only logical that they should act as poor men. The resultant hardship could be offered in satisfaction for those who had surrounded themselves with every luxury while leading lives of vice.

So, in the bright October days of the year 1220, Hyacinth and Henry trudged steadily northeast, stopping occasionally to preach and to exhort the people to more intense Christian living. And everywhere they went—in upper and lower Austria, in Slovakia and Moravia—they found themselves warmly greeted and made the center of attraction. For none of the inhabitants had ever seen preaching friars, and over and over again Hyacinth was forced to refuse hospitable offers to stay a while in this city or that. But presently the citizens of Olmütz, a town one hundred and twenty-five miles southwest of Cracow, would not be denied. They had just learned that Brother Henry was one of themselves—a native of Moravia. It was not to be thought of that he should go on to Cracow when his own Czech people needed preachers so much.

"The young man tells us he is almost ready to

be ordained a priest," said the mayor of Olmütz. "Oh, Father Hyacinth! Couldn't you leave him with us? We would build a convent for the novices who are already flocking to him! And a church and school! Oh, just look about and see the fine things Brother Henry could do here for God and souls!"

Hyacinth was puzzled. Over five months ago he had left Rome with three companions, presumably to work in Poland. But how many times his plans had been changed! First Herman had been taken from him to guide the destiny of the convent at Friesach. Then Bishop Andreas had called for preaching friars, and so Ceslaus had gone to Prague. Now in Olmütz God was asking for still another sacrifice: the return of Hyacinth to Poland without a fellow-religious, without any link to those happy days as a novice in Santa Sabina!

"Not my will but Thine be done!" he murmured after a moment's hesitation. Then, turning to the mayor, he made a little gesture toward Henry.

Immediately the official's eyes brightened. "You mean it, Father?" he cried eagerly. "Brother Henry may stay here with us?"

Hyacinth gave a deep sigh. "Yes. He may stay," he said.

So presently Henry was kneeling for a blessing, while the population of Olmütz went wild with excitement. It was true! Brother Henry had been given permission to receive novices into the Order. The civil authorities had turned over a large building to serve as a temporary convent, and there would be a week's delay in Hyacinth's departure for

Cracow. During this interval there would be sermons every morning in the public square.

As at Friesach, great marvels of conversion were soon being wrought by Hyacinth's preaching. The secular clergy were called upon to administer the Sacraments to such unusual crowds that soon word was going around that the Polish priest was a saint. By a single glance he could instill sorrow for sin in a hardened heart, break the strangling hold of one lifelong temptation after another, then show that men may experience true peace in this world only in proportion to the manner in which they know, love and do the Holy Will of God.

"And Father Hyacinth cures not only sick souls but sick bodies as well!" cried a young mother, half beside herself with joy. "My boy was blind from birth, but look at him now! Why, he sees like any normal child!"

"Yes, and my husband's well again, too!" put in another woman joyfully. "He's been lame for years, but yesterday Father Hyacinth prayed over him, and now his twisted leg is straight. Oh, thank God for sending such a wonderful man to us!"

As was only natural, there was ultimately the same difficulty in Olmütz as there had been in Friesach. The people did not want Hyacinth to leave. With tears and sobs they entreated him to continue with his preaching. But duty had long been calling him to Poland, and when the week was up he gave his last sermon, blessed the huge crowds, then made his way slowly through the public square and down the principal street. At his side walked Brother Henry, his face anxious and drawn.

"How is it you can leave me alone so soon, Father?" he kept asking piteously. "After all, you stayed in Friesach for several months, so that the convent was well established when you left Brother Herman in charge. But here. . ."

Hyacinth nodded cheerfully. "I know. Here I have stayed only a week. And you have had almost no advice on the duties of a Prior. Yet remember this, my son: you are not timid and slow at books, as was our good Brother Herman. The Lord has given you a quick mind and a wonderful power to understand troubled hearts. You are a leader by nature, Brother Henry, and so I have seen fit to guide you in another way. From the start I would have you lean upon God instead of upon me."

Despite his natural sorrow in saying good-bye, Henry recognized the wisdom in his superior's words. Yes—if only people would lean upon God instead of upon creatures there would be far fewer disappointments in the world, far less heartbreak over human frailty!

"I. . .I will try to lean upon God," he whispered. "I will put my work as Prior completely into His hands and do my best not to worry. But you will remember me in prayer, won't you, Father? I *know* I will need much help not to weaken, once I am left alone."

For the last time Hyacinth raised his hand in fatherly blessing. "I will never forget you," he promised. "And be of good heart, Brother Henry. Doing God's Will can never be cause for real sorrow, no matter how hard it is. For God's Will implies perfection, without any stain of sin, and this can mean only one thing for us if we are wise enough to accept it—*lasting happiness someday in Heaven!*"

With these words Hyacinth took his departure from Olmütz and from the last of his original companions. But during the next few days, as he plodded steadily northeast, he found as much comfort in the brief message of farewell as Brother Henry had done. God's Will! How true that its acceptance or rejection decides the fate of every man, woman and child living in the world!

"I must try to spread this truth in Cracow," he thought. "Surely if only ten people can be led to believe it, there will be a change for the better in many other hearts."

The opportunity to preach to his fellow-countrymen was not far away. Early on the morning of the Feast of All Saints, Hyacinth knew that he would be with his friends and loved ones before nightfall. Yes—Cracow was now only a few miles distant, and as he walked swiftly across the rolling plains toward the Vistula, Hyacinth's heart beat fast with excitement. Assuredly Bishop Ivo had arranged for him to live near the Cathedral. Since this was in a central part of the city, it would be an excellent place to preach and instruct. Then, if God so willed, a few young Poles would apply for admission into the Order. A monastery would be built, possibly even a convent for nuns, for had not Father Dominic often said that preaching without prayer and sacrifice behind it is of little use to souls?

"My cousin Bronislava would be interested in that statement," he thought. "She has been a Norbertine nun since 1217—over three years. And I know she has always prayed very earnestly that Ceslaus and I would be successful as preachers."

So lost was Hyacinth in his thoughts that at first he did not notice a boy and girl gathering fallen branches in a pine grove near the road. The two youngsters called out to him to stop, then shouldered their burdens and ran after him eagerly. Who was he? they wanted to know. Why was he wearing a robe of white wool with a black cloak about his shoulders? Was this the way people dressed in some far-away country?

"Little friends, I'm Father Hyacinth," he told them, smiling. "My clothes are those of a Friar Preacher, and I've come from Rome to Cracow with important news for souls. Now, who are you?"

"My name is Stanislaus," announced the boy promptly. "I'm ten years old, and I live a mile farther down this road."

"And I'm his sister Elizabeth," said the girl. "I'm eight years old. Every day we gather wood for our parents."

Hyacinth nodded approvingly. Both Stanislaus and Elizabeth had the fair hair and blue eyes that were so common in Poland. Their plain homespun garb and the confident manner in which they carried their burdens of firewood showed that they were of the peasant class—sturdy and accustomed to hard work out-of-doors. But suddenly the friar's glance narrowed. Could it be that something was wrong? That the two children. . .

It surprised the youngsters when their new friend suddenly suggested that he carry the bundles of wood. Apparently he wanted to hear more about both brother and sister and believed that talking would be easier for the children if they did not have such awkward loads upon their shoulders.

"I do like your names," he told them, smiling. "Stanislaus and Elizabeth. Of course you received them in Baptism?"

Elizabeth's blue eyes widened. "In Baptism?" she asked curiously. "What's that?"

A sudden pain shot through Hyacinth's heart. So—his fears had not been groundless! These children, like hundreds of thousands of others in northern Europe, had never been baptized. Neither, probably, had their parents or grandparents. Indeed, young Stanislaus probably knew nothing of the man who had made this name the holiest in Poland's history—Bishop Stanislaus of Cracow—in 1079 the country's first martyr at the wicked hands of King Boleslaus the Second. As for the little girl—had anyone ever told her of the Blessed Virgin or of her cousin Elizabeth?

So it was that presently Hyacinth was giving the peasant children their first lesson in Catechism. They listened attentively, for never before had they heard anyone speak of Heaven, that wonderful place where men and women live in eternal glory after having served God faithfully upon earth.

"You mean that we can go to Heaven, too, Father Hyacinth?" asked Elizabeth, her eyes shining. "We can go there, even if we're poor?"

The friar smiled. "Yes, child. God wishes all the souls He has made to be happy with Him forever in Heaven. But they must love and serve Him in the way He has told us."

The little girl was on the point of asking still more questions when suddenly her brother seized her arm. "What luck, Elizabeth! See the big procession? The Duke must be coming out from the city!"

Immediately the child forgot her new-found interest in the next world. Shading her eyes, she stood on tip-toe and gazed spellbound into the distance. For the road they had been traveling had now reached its highest point. Cracow lay before them, and the blue waters of the Vistula, while winding out from the city's south gate were more than fifty carriages decked with gay banners and flags!

Elizabeth tugged eagerly at Hyacinth's cloak. "Look, Father! The gold and scarlet carriage with the twelve white horses belongs to Duke Leszek. Isn't it beautiful?"

Hyacinth smiled. "Yes, child. And we have a wonderful view from here."

Suddenly Stanislaus let out an excited squeal. "Two soldiers are riding ahead, Father, and waving at us! Do you suppose that means we should get off the road?"

The friar shifted the two bundles of firewood on

his shoulders. His keen eyes had just identified the coat-of-arms of Bishop Ivo flying from one of the carriages. With a little laugh he looked down at the boy beside him.

"No, I don't think we need to get off the road, Stanislaus."

"But the Duke must be coming to greet some important visitor! A prince, maybe! Or a king!"

Again Hyacinth laughed. "No, little friend. I believe this visitor is as poor as any beggar in Cracow."

CHAPTER 7

THE WORK BEGINS

A FEW minutes later the brilliant procession had halted at a short distance down the road and dozens of noblemen and clerics were emerging from the carriages. What was the children's amazement when they observed that the attention of the entire company was upon the man who was laden with their own bundles of firewood! Then, before their eyes, Leszek the White, Duke of Cracow, approached Hyacinth and prostrated himself in the dust. And thus he lay until the friar had raised him to his feet.

"Your Grace, I am only a human being," Hyacinth protested. "I deserve no such reception as this."

Leszek's face was pale as he pointed a trembling hand toward the sky. "But surely you saw her, Father?"

"Saw whom, Your Grace?"

"Why, the Blessed Virgin! A few minutes ago it was as if the heavens had opened. I saw Our Lady standing in the clouds, and she was giving you her

"I SAW OUR LADY STANDING IN THE CLOUDS!"

blessing. It was before her loveliness that I threw myself in the dust."

At these words a murmur of astonishment ran through the crowd and all eyes looked upwards. But soon it was evident that the vision had lasted just a few seconds and that it had been seen by Leszek only. Apparently God wished that the Duke of Cracow should appreciate Hyacinth's entrance into the city and do all that he could to help the Friar Preacher in his missionary labors among the Poles.

In the weeks that followed, Leszek and the other lords and nobles spared no effort to make Hyacinth welcome and to further his work in all possible ways. Before long it had become evident that the house near the Cathedral which Bishop Ivo had turned over to him was far too small. Already thirty young men from the better families of Cracow had applied for admission as friars. A convent and also a really large church would be necessary if vocations continued to increase.

"Cracow has only two churches, the Cathedral and the Church of the Holy Trinity," said Bishop Ivo one day, smiling fondly at his nephew. "Did you know that we have decided to give you the latter, my son? The Duke, the nobles, the clergy—everyone is in favor of your having it. But of course it will have to be remodeled and a convent attached. The work will probably take a year or two to finish and will be paid for by voluntary offerings. The Duke has promised to make the first donation."

Hyacinth's eyes shone. A church of the Friars Preachers in Cracow! How wonderful!

"Uncle Ivo, how can I thank you?" he murmured. "Day by day it seems that wonders follow one another; and just when things grow hard, then God lightens the load with an unexpected joy like this. Oh, I shall be so happy to have Holy Trinity for a church! When you see the Duke, tell him that God will reward his generosity far more than he dreams possible."

Thus it was that early in the year 1221 repairs and alterations began upon the Church and Monastery of the Holy Trinity. Hyacinth's thirty novices, who had succeeded in crowding into the house which Bishop Ivo had given him, always welcomed the little outings which their beloved Father Prior arranged—but more especially now, when these frequently included a tour of their future home. What a delight to walk through the cells, the Chapter Hall, the refectory—to hear Hyacinth speak of his own life as a novice in the beautiful Monastery of Santa Sabina in Rome, of Father Dominic de Guzman, the Spanish preacher who had founded their Order!

"How I wish Father Dominic could come here and see our new convent," said Brother Florian one day. "Do you suppose it could be arranged, Father Hyacinth?"

Hyacinth looked intently at the young speaker, then turned away abruptly. "No, Brother. It can never be arranged."

There was such a strained quality in Hyacinth's voice that Brother Florian was worried. Had he done wrong to ask the question? If so, he was truly sorry and would make amends. But as he sought to express such feelings, Hyacinth placed a kindly hand upon his arm.

"No, my son. It's all right. The question was quite in order. Only it startled me just a little. You see, last night God let me understand that Father Dominic is now with Him in Heaven. Never again, at least in this world, shall I see my dear Father and friend."

Last night—August 6, 1221! The novices looked at one another in consternation, not so much at the news of Father Dominic's death as at their Father Hyacinth's calm statement that he had learned of it by miraculous means. Surely it was true then— what people said—that he was a saint?

At the sight of thirty young faces somber and not a little fearful, Hyacinth smiled broadly. "My sons, the death of one who served God faithfully should never cause sadness. Come—I'll tell you a little more of Father Dominic and the wonderful things he did for souls in the South."

So once again the novices gathered to hear the story of how Dominic had founded his religious family. Now, after some fifteen years, it consisted of three types of members. The first group was that of the preaching friars and lay Brothers; the second, that of the cloistered nuns. Both groups, or Orders, were bound by vow to God's service. But gradually there had come into being another group. This Third Order consisted of lay people—men and women living in the world, both married and single. These made no vows in the strict religious sense, but they did promise to lead more prayerful lives, to fast on certain days and to perform other small sacrifices. Throughout life these members of the Third Order would share in the merits of the preaching friars, the lay Brothers and the cloistered nuns. At death they could be buried in the full religious habit. Always they would be remembered in the prayers and good works of the entire Order.

"As you know, my own mother and grandmother are members of the Third Order," concluded Hyacinth happily. "My sons, when you are ready to go out to preach, do all you can to promote this way of life among the people. It will mean so much to them."

Hyacinth's reputation for holiness increased steadily in Cracow. All agreed that there had never been such a wonderful preacher in the city. Why, he was on fire with love for sinners, and his sermons at the Cathedral produced the most amazing conversions! For instance, were there souls who could not tear themselves away from a certain sin? who hated their neighbor? who possessed ill-gotten goods? who had received the Sacraments unworthily? Let them listen to Father Hyacinth for five minutes, and before the day was over they would be kneeling at his feet and making a good Confession.

"I think God is really pleased with our country," Duke Leszek confided to Bishop Ivo one day. "We did not receive the Faith until the tenth century. Now, in the thirteenth, one or more of our young men come to Father Hyacinth each week and ask to be received into his Order."

The Bishop smiled, then shook his head at the trace of smugness in the Duke's voice. "You know there is more to Poland than the city of Cracow, Your Grace—or a few dozen youths who seek to enter a monastery. We mustn't forget that the way to Heaven is the Way of the Cross—for a single soul or for an entire nation."

The Duke's eyes narrowed. "You mean..."

"I mean that during this past year Father Hyacinth has only been sowing the seed, and in one city. We must wait a while for the real harvest."

"Then Father Hyacinth will have to leave us for other cities?"

"Why not, Your Grace? Sandomierz is calling for him right now, and Troppau. We must never try to keep him to ourselves. That would only be selfish."

The Duke nodded slowly, while an expression of bewilderment crept into his eyes. "You mentioned that the Way of the Cross is the only way to Heaven," he said. "Bishop Ivo, surely that isn't true? Surely there must be some easier way to reach God than that of suffering?"

The Bishop hesitated. Only that morning he had had a long talk with Hyacinth, and the friar had spoken out plainly on this very point. He had begun with a description of Paradise, the Place of Perfection where Adam and Eve had been free to enjoy the good things God had created for them. There had been no fear, pain or ugliness here until the dreadful moment when pride entered the hearts of our First Parents and they considered the Devil's tempting suggestion that by eating of the forbidden fruit they might become God's equal and hence not be required to obey Him.

"Can you believe it?" cried the Bishop incredulously. "Two creatures made by God out of the slime of the earth dared to think that they could be equal to *Him!*"

Leszek was silent. What did all this have to do with going to Heaven by the Way of the Cross?

Ivo sensed the unspoken question and quickly resumed his story, pointing out the terrible disappointment which awaited Adam and Eve after they had disobeyed the Heavenly Father. For instead of being equal to their Creator, they were now even less than they had been. Indeed, they were much inferior to those two splendid human creatures over whom sickness and death had never had any power. Suddenly a dreadful germ had lodged within them—the germ of sin. Henceforth they must carry this germ about with them, and their children must carry it, too. Henceforth the human understanding would be darkened and the will weakened, so that frequently men and women would find it much easier to do evil than to do good. And this germ of sin (that is, this weakness) would be in every body as well as in every soul, so that eventually all mankind would become prey to sickness and death.

"Actually, this was the beginning of man's Way of the Cross," said the Bishop thoughtfully. "You see, from the moment Adam and Eve sinned against God they became unfit for Paradise. As part of their punishment they had to leave the Garden and go

through life as we know it now. They had to learn
the meaning of pain and work. They had to look
into their children's eyes and know that henceforth
each soul born into the world would have to remain
away from God, from the joys of Heaven, because
it carried within it the stain of Original Sin. Even
death would not change matters, for in Limbo there
would still be a separation from God."

"Yes, but Christ died on Calvary and redeemed
Adam and Eve and every other soul for Heaven,"
put in the Duke quickly. "He paid for Original Sin
by the most dreadful suffering. Why wasn't this
suffering enough? Why do you say that the only way
to Heaven, for a single soul or for an entire nation,
is by the Way of the Cross?"

The Bishop hesitated. There were several
answers to this very important question, but he
would give the Duke the one that had always
appealed to him most.

"Christ did win back for us the privilege of
entering Paradise," he conceded. "His sufferings
and death were more than sufficient to atone for
Original Sin. But you see, Your Grace, we are still
children of Adam and Eve, and most imperfect.
Even if we had the chance to go to Paradise now,
we could not bear to do so."

"What?"

"That's right. Paradise is a Place of Perfection,
and we can never want to enter it until we ourselves
are perfect. And we can become perfect only by
doing what Adam and Eve were too proud to do."

"What's that?"

"Uniting ourselves to the Will of the Heavenly Father in all things—which means never questioning, even for an instant, the events He places in our daily lives. Or, to put it in another way, accepting His Will as completely as Christ accepted it when He lived on earth."

"*So that's what you mean by the Way of the Cross!*"

"Yes, Your Grace. And those who follow it faithfully in this world will never have to go to Purgatory. They will have been made perfect here."

For a moment Duke Leszek was silent. Then he gave a deep sigh. "How wonderful to be able to live by this doctrine!" he said slowly. "But surely it is too sublime for the average man?"

The Bishop smiled. "Saint Stanislaus could change your mind on that score," he said. "After all, he is in glory today because of the Way of the Cross. Why don't you ask him for help?"

In the weeks that followed, Leszek was faithful to the Bishop's suggestion. No day passed that he did not kneel in the royal chapel and beg Saint Stanislaus for the grace to live completely united to God's Will. And he was not alone in his devotion. Of late Hyacinth had aroused an increased popular interest in Poland's first martyr, and presently it was announced that the holy relics would be moved. For generations they had been venerated in the village of Skalka, on the other side of the Vistula. Now they were to be enshrined in a more fitting resting place in the Cathedral of Cracow. The ceremony of translation would take place on December 27, 1221.

On the morning of the great day, Hyacinth set out for the river bank with his entire community. The streets were crowded, for the Duke and his nobles, the Bishop and the secular clergy, men and women from all walks of life, were scheduled to cross the Vistula and then go in pilgrimage to Skalka. There was excitement everywhere as friend greeted friend, but Hyacinth took no note of familiar faces as he made his way through the streets behind his youthful friars. Rather, he gave himself up to prayer—and with good reason, for this morning in the little chapel of Skalka he was to preach the principal sermon on Bishop Stanislaus.

Some minutes later, however, as he entered the boat that was to take him across the river, a distraction occurred. Stanislaus was called "Saint" by everyone, Hyacinth reflected; yet actually he had never been canonized. How wonderful if the Friars Preachers could work to place him among the officially recognized heroes of the Church!

"I'm sure Father Dominic would approve," he told himself. "Yes, if he were in my place, I'm positive he would do everything he could to make Bishop Stanislaus known and loved."

But fascinating as this thought was, the time was hardly fitting to dwell upon it, and so Hyacinth dutifully returned to his meditation upon the great Polish martyr. In his mind he rehearsed the account which he must give of the Bishop's life:

Stanislaus was born in 1030. He was a good and learned man and finally became Bishop of Cracow. He tried to show King Boleslaus the Second that even kings must be subject to God and His authority. They must have only one wife at a time; they must not steal or lie or be cruel in battle. But Boleslaus was not easily taught, and the day came when Stanislaus found himself faced with a dangerous situation. The King had been leading a wicked life, laughing openly at the Commandments, and now he falsely accused the Bishop of not paying for a certain piece of land which he had bought in the name of the Church. What could be done to put a stop to such scandals?

Excommunication! The very word sent a chill through Hyacinth's veins. Yes, after many warnings, Stanislaus finally had to excommunicate the King. But instead of then seeing the light, Boleslaus became consumed with anger. He ordered his soldiers to go to the Bishop's palace and kill him. Three stalwart men were chosen, but at the critical moment their courage failed. They could not raise their swords against the kindly Bishop. Then Boleslaus went himself. He found Stanislaus at the altar, in the act of offering the Holy Sacrifice of the Mass, but even this did not deter him. With one swing of his sword he struck off the Bishop's head. The date was May 8, 1079, and Stanislaus was forty-nine years old.

"Father Hyacinth!" cried the faraway voice of young Brother Benedict. "Father Hyacinth!"

The friar looked up. Why, the trip across the river had been made in a far shorter time than usual! At least half of the boats were across, and the banks were crowded with pilgrims. It was a colorful scene, but Hyacinth's eyes passed quickly over it, seeking Brother Benedict.

"Yes, I called you," said the latter, suddenly emerging from the crowd and stretching out a hand to help his Father Prior ashore. "Oh, Father, something terrible has happened! Can you come quickly, please?"

Hyacinth leaped from the boat. "Of course. What's wrong?"

Brother Benedict pointed a few yards down the river bank. A little group of women was gathered here, and one of them was crying as though her heart would break.

"Her name is Falislava, Father. She's a widow, and her only son was drowned last night while he was trying to cross the river. See? There's a fisherman bringing in the body to shore now."

As Hyacinth raised his hand in sympathetic blessing, there was a sudden wail. Falislava, half-crazed with grief, had just learned of his arrival.

"Oh, help me, Father!" she sobbed, stumbling through the curious crowds and collapsing at his feet. "Give me back my boy!"

CHAPTER 8

TWO PROMISES

THERE WAS no doubt about it. Falislava really believed that the celebrated preacher from Cracow could work a miracle. Kneeling at his feet, weary and bedraggled after an all-night vigil at the water's edge, she renewed her heart-rending pleas.

"I'm a widow, Father Hyacinth! Peter was my only son. Oh, in God's Name, bring him back to me!"

There was real tragedy here, and for the second time Hyacinth raised his hand in blessing over the anguished mother. Then he knelt down beside the lifeless body which had just been placed before him. Gently he examined it, then winced. Peter had been a handsome youth—strong and well-proportioned—in the very springtime of life.

As he prayed for the dead boy, Hyacinth recalled that day nearly two years ago when Father Dominic had restored life to the young nephew of Cardinal Orsini. When everyone had urged him to pray that the laws of nature might be set aside, the Saint had

at first hesitated; but after offering the Holy Sacrifice, he had ordered Napoleon to rise from death,
in the Name of Jesus Christ.

"Oh, Father. . .Father. . ." moaned Falislava
brokenly, mistaking the friar's thoughtfulness for
lack of interest in her sorrow.

Hyacinth reached out a comforting hand, then
sighed and turned away. Alas! What could he do—
he, who was only an unworthy follower of Dominic?
Yet perhaps if it were a question of giving glory to
God. . .of renewing the faith of this crowd of pilgrims. . .Hyacinth's heart almost stopped beating
at the thought.

Suddenly he reached down and took the youth's
stiffened hand in his. "Peter, may Our Lord Jesus
Christ, Whose glory I preach, give you back life
through the intercession of the Blessed Virgin
Mary!"

The words rang out clearly on the crisp December air, but before their full meaning could be
grasped, a great cry burst from the crowd. Falislava's son, who had been cold in death for almost
twenty-four hours, stirred, then raised himself. In
a moment his mother was eagerly embracing him.

Immediately all thoughts of Saint Stanislaus and
the proposed pilgrimage to Skalka were forgotten.
Almost hysterical with joy, men and women
pressed about Hyacinth to kiss his hand, to touch
his habit, to implore his blessing upon themselves
and their families. Never had they witnessed such
a wonder as this, and even Hyacinth's youngest
followers came in for a share of praise. Surely they

were not far from being saints themselves, these
boys who wore the black and white habit of the
Order of Friars Preachers? After all, didn't they
live with Father Hyacinth? Weren't they being
trained by him?

For nearly an hour, joyful confusion reigned
along the banks of the Vistula, but finally Hyacinth
succeeded in restoring calm. In a voice filled with
emotion he implored the pilgrims to cease their
childish reverence of him. It was only fitting that
the recent miracle should be attributed to Saint
Stanislaus, rather than to a poor preaching friar.

"Oh, my friends!" he cried, tears glistening in his
eyes. "There is only one explanation for this morning's marvel. God wishes us to recognize His power,
the glory of His saints. He wishes that we give ourselves to Him completely, so that He may return
our poor gift by the gift of Himself. Then, when
He is in our hearts, how easy it will be to understand the true meaning of love!"

The crowd was settling itself for a sermon, over-
joyed at the privilege of feasting its eyes upon a
wonderworker, when suddenly Hyacinth motioned
to his friars and began to move away from the river
bank. Others might have forgotten Saint Stanislaus,
but not he. This very minute many hundreds were
waiting at the Cathedral in Cracow for the arrival
of the holy relics. Therefore, the pilgrimage to
Skalka ought to get underway at once.

Naturally the story of Peter's restoration to life
soon brought the holy preacher increased fame.
Before another year had passed there were also

PETER WAS NO LONGER DEAD!

new wonders to report. On May 30, 1222, Father Hyacinth had cured a woman stricken with paralysis and for more than six weeks unable to speak. On September 30 of the same year his prayers had cured a second woman—this one driven to insanity by severe headaches. There were also other favors—less spectacular, perhaps, but nonetheless authentic—and as he entered upon his third year of priestly labor for souls in Cracow, Hyacinth knew that he possessed the people's universal love and respect. Due to a special gift from God, he had not a single enemy in the entire city.

Early in the year 1223, repairs and alterations upon the Monastery and Church of the Holy Trinity were finally completed, and it was announced that on March 25, the Feast of the Annunciation, the Order of Friars Preachers would take over its new property. There would be a solemn ceremony of dedication then, and all buildings would be opened to the public. By a special dispensation even women would be allowed inside the cloister.

Among the celebrities who thronged to Holy Trinity on the morning of the great day was Gregory Crescentius, an Italian Cardinal who had been sent to Poland as Papal Legate by Honorius the Third. With him was his nephew and secretary, Father James. The latter had been ordained at a very early age in Rome, having made a brilliant record there as a student. Now he was in his middle twenties, and those who knew of his extraordinary mental powers predicted that someday he would be appointed a Bishop—perhaps even a Cardinal!

"This young priest has one of the finest minds in Rome," they told one another. "His uncle does right to be proud of him."

Father James, although he was truly interested in the welfare of souls, was not displeased at the prospect of rising to an important position in Church circles. Of course he knew that his friends were not infallible. There was every chance that he might never be a Bishop at all, for some dreadful illness might come upon him, or some accident, so that he would be unable to assume the responsible post. Still, there was also the chance that if he did satisfactory work in Poland as his uncle's secretary, in time he would be recalled to Rome. Then, God willing, the Holy Father would take him aside. . .would congratulate him upon a task well done. . .would speak the wonderful words that meant promotion to a more important role in God's Church. . .

Such thoughts filled the mind of Father James as he and his Cardinal-uncle took their places in the Church of the Holy Trinity. It was a cold and blustery day in Cracow, with the ground still blanketed in snow. Indeed, travel by sleigh was still necessary in the city's outskirts. Yet seven hundred and fifty miles to the southwest it must be a vastly different story, James told himself. By now spring ought to have arrived in Italy. The trees should be in bud along the highways, with violets and other early blossoms gracing the sheltered gardens of his father's house. Oh, it would be good to be in Rome again—to hear the soft music of his native tongue, to visit the splendid churches and shrines of the greatest city in the world...

Suddenly there was a ripple of excitement at the back of the church, and everyone realized that Father Hyacinth was arriving with his community. In a moment he and his friars would come in procession up the center aisle and into the sanctuary, where Bishop Ivo, attended by the canons of the Cathedral, was already awaiting him. Then formal presentation of the church and monastery would be made, after which Hyacinth would offer the Holy Sacrifice of the Mass. Later he would mount to the pulpit and express his gratitude in a special sermon. After this, clergy and laity would join in the singing of the *Te Deum* and repair to the monastery for a tour of inspection.

With the rest of the congregation, Father James arose as the procession entered the church. He was feeling quite as usual and readily joined in the familiar chant of the Litany of the Saints. But as the double line of black-and-white-clad friars made its way into the sanctuary, led by the youngest novices, his heart began to pound in a disturbing fashion. Turning slightly, he saw that Hyacinth was bringing up the rear—a peaceful smile upon his lips, an unearthly radiance in his eyes. And as James looked into those eyes, a strange thing happened. Suddenly it was as though Cracow's holy preacher were a magnet and he but a helpless piece of steel.

"Come, my son," the friar seemed to say. "Come and serve God as He wills you should serve Him."

The rest of the morning passed like a dream.

Father James assisted at Mass as well as he could and listened to Hyacinth's burning words, but all the while it seemed as though he were living outside of his body. Occasionally his uncle inquired as to whether or not he was feeling well, whereupon James promptly returned to himself. Yes, yes. Of course he was feeling well. Why not? Yet extraordinary words kept repeating themselves within his brain, words he had never thought to hear.

"You're going to be a Friar Preacher. Before the day is over, you'll have asked Father Hyacinth to give you the habit."

James could scarcely believe this; yet he knew it must be true. Suddenly God's grace was sweeping into him with such force that it seemed useless to resist. Already a priest, he now would consecrate his life to an even higher degree by becoming a religious. Yes—he would give up all rights to personal possessions, to the esteem and glory he might enjoy if he remained in the world. He would even pronounce a vow of obedience to a fellow human being and thus make a really complete offering of himself to God.

There was general consternation when the news was learned. Indeed, Duke Leszek, the nobles, the secular clergy, even Bishop Ivo, were not too sure that James was doing the right thing. As for Gregory Crescentius, Papal Legate and uncle of the young man, he was thoroughly convinced that the whole affair was a dreadful mistake.

"Why, you haven't the health to lead the life of a friar!" he declared flatly. "Think of the many fast days! The rising in the middle of the night to chant the Office! Oh, James! You're not used to such hardships!"

The young priest agreed. But why couldn't such a lack be remedied in his case as it had been for others? And as for not possessing sufficient strength for the new life—well, wasn't that really a matter for God to decide?

"There's no use in arguing, Uncle," he concluded gently. "My mind is made up. If Father Hyacinth is willing to have me, I'm going to be a friar."

Naturally Hyacinth was willing. Before another week was underway, he had received James into the community. And with real joy, for Heaven had seen fit to enlighten him as to the young Italian's future. At this moment he knew that someday this new friar would do great things for souls. He would go to Constantinople and guide the destiny of a convent of Friars Preachers there. Eventually he would become Provincial of the Order in Poland, succeeding Father Gerard and Father Ceslaus in this most important post.

As time passed, other young men were received by Hyacinth into the new monastery. Indeed, by the year 1224 he was able to make the second foundation of the Order in Poland. This was at Sandomierz, about one hundred miles northeast of Cracow. At the same time plans were completed for the establishment of a third monastery—this one at Troppau, one hundred miles west of the city.

The holy preacher was happy as he realized that at last he was spreading the Faith in Poland. But

even as his heart rejoiced, he knew that there were
other and more difficult missionary fields awaiting
laborers. For instance, what about Prussia, that wild
and dangerous country that bordered on the Baltic
Sea? Then surely there were possibilities in Denmark, Sweden, Norway. . .

"Dearest Mother, please give me the grace to
work in these lands!" he often prayed. "Let me
help many there to know your Son—to love Him
and to do His Will!"

On August 15, 1224, the Feast of the Assumption, Hyacinth was in the Church of the Holy
Trinity at Cracow. It was about two o'clock in the
morning, and the friars had just finished chanting
Matins and Lauds. As they withdrew to their cells
to resume their sleep, Hyacinth remained where he
was—thinking on the meaning of Our Lady's
Assumption.

"Oh, Blessed Mother, you lived in this world
about sixty years. Then God called you to Himself.
But instead of allowing your body to turn to dust
in the earth, He sent angels to carry it to Heaven.
Oh, Mother, how wonderful! This very minute your
body is in glory, completely perfect. You didn't have
to wait until the Last Day, as we poor sinners must
do. . ."

Hyacinth's eyes were closed as he prayed, so that
at first he was unaware that a strange and glorious
light was surrounding the statue of the Blessed
Mother near the main altar. But suddenly he looked
up, and then his heart all but stopped for joy. Why,
the Queen of Heaven was standing before him! In

the form of a young woman dressed in white and gold, she had taken the place of the statue and now was smiling upon him tenderly!

"Rejoice, Hyacinth," she said, and her voice was like the sweetest music. "Your prayers are pleasing to my Son. From now on all that you ask of Him in my name will be granted."

The friar scarcely dared to move. Oh, how beautiful she was—the Blessed Virgin! How motherly! How kind! And suddenly he knew that he must speak, too. He must ask for the extraordinary favor he had long kept hidden in his heart.

"Dearest Mother, please hear me," he whispered. "I want a certain grace so much...a favor..."

The vision smiled encouragingly. "Yes? What is it?"

With sudden abandonment Hyacinth flung out his arms to Heaven's Queen. "Oh, Mother, I want to bring the True Faith to *all* of northern Europe! Yes, and I want to take it to Russia, too! Will you bless my efforts? Will you give me the necessary strength?"

For a moment all was quiet in the deserted church. Then the Blessed Mother smiled. "My Son has just granted this favor," she said, pointing to the Tabernacle. "Oh, Hyacinth, because you have loved me and sought my help, you will do even more for souls than you imagine! But in return, I would ask a favor, too."

The friar stared. Our Lady would ask a *favor?* And from *him?* Surely this wasn't possible! Still...

"You know I'll do anything you ask," he hastened

to answer. "Just tell me what it is, Mother."

The vision smiled. "My favor is this, Hyacinth: *Bring me souls! Teach them to look upon me as a true mother! Describe the great graces God lets me give to all who ask my help!*"

The friar nodded slowly. Of course he would make this promise. From now on he would never let pass an opportunity to spread devotion to the Mother of God. Wherever he preached, he would tell of her kindness, her love for souls. It was little enough to do in return for the wonderful promise she herself had just made: that someday he would be a missionary to all of northern Europe—and even to Russia!

CHAPTER 9

THE WORK CONTINUES

IT WAS three years later when Cracow's famous preacher finally began the second phase of his life's work: namely, the Christianizing of northern Europe. By now the Monastery of the Holy Trinity was firmly established, and he had no scruples about placing Father Gerard in charge. He was an able man and would do good work as Prior. He would also see that the daughter houses at Sandomierz and Troppau continued to prosper.

"As for us, we can now go to Prussia with a clear conscience," said Hyacinth thankfully. "Aren't you pleased, my sons?"

Brothers Florian, Godinus and Benedict—the young religious who had been chosen by Hyacinth as his companions—nodded quickly. "Oh, yes, Father!" they cried with one voice. "Thank you so much for letting us come with you!"

Yet, as they trudged steadily northward, the three young men sometimes found themselves uneasy. Although they had never been to Prussia, they were not ignorant of the real dangers there for a stranger.

For instance, the country lay along the Baltic Sea, between the mouths of the Vistula and the Memel rivers, and was almost cut off from the outside world by dense forests and gloomy swamps. Pagan tribes lived in the forests and swamps, eking out a livelihood as hunters and fishermen. There were no sizeable towns or cities, no real civilization, since the Prussians did not enjoy agricultural pursuits and never stayed long in one place. Somehow they could not find any satisfaction in clearing a piece of land, tilling it, sowing it, then waiting for a harvest that frequently never came because of drought, wind, hail or frost. Oh, no! It was much more exciting to be on the move, hunting the wild boars and deer through valleys and woods.

"They say the Prussians are the most hardened warriors and have killed those missionaries who tried to change their ways," Florian confided to Benedict one morning. "Adalbert of Prague, for instance. And Bruno of Querfurt..."

Benedict shivered. "I know. I learned the story of Saint Adalbert when I was a boy. As I remember it, he became Archbishop of Gniezno, worked many years among the Prussians, then died a martyr at their hands."

Florian nodded. "That's right. The Prussians killed Adalbert in 997, and King Boleslaus the First ransomed his body by giving the murderers an equal weight in gold. But that's over two hundred years ago, Benedict. Don't you suppose things have changed for the better since then?"

The latter shook his head. "Father Hyacinth says

the Prussians are still pagans and very cruel. It will take much hard work to convert them."

So that his young friends might have a little more courage for their hazardous journey, Hyacinth finally told them of Our Lady's visit and of her promise to be with him in all his missionary labors.

"Don't you see now that we simply can't fail?" he asked cheerfully. "As far as that goes, maybe we shouldn't bother too much with Prussia on this trip. What do you think of the idea of visiting Pomerania first?"

Brother Godinus stared incredulously, for in his mind's eye he had already seen himself a martyr at the hands of the Prussians. "But Pomerania is hardly a pagan country, Father Hyacinth! Didn't Bishop Otto of Bamberg convert it over a hundred years ago?"

"Yes, what work could we do there?" added Florian.

Hyacinth smiled. "I know that much of Pomerania has received the Faith, my sons. But it seems to me that it would be a good thing for us to secure the friendship of Duke Swientopelk. He's the country's leader, you know, and if he allows us to build a convent in Pomerania, then we'll have a really good chance to bring the Faith to the Prussians. After all, they are Pomerania's neighbors—just across the Vistula to the east."

Although the young religious knew that their opinions could mean little, since they themselves were so inexperienced, they also knew that Father Hyacinth expected an answer to his suggestion. So first Benedict spoke up, then Florian and Godinus. Solemnly all agreed that it would be well to go to Pomerania first and afterwards to Prussia.

"Then that's what we'll do," said Hyacinth. "And when we've had our interview with Duke Swiento-pelk, we'll take a little trip to the Cistercian Abbey of Oliva and meet Abbot Christian and his monks. These good men have done wonders for souls in the North and they'll be glad to help us with prayers and advice."

As a result of this and other little talks, the young friars found themselves growing in courage. As day followed day, they plunged steadily northward through forest and swamp in the direction of Pomerania. But despite their superior's cheering words, there were times when all three looked despairingly at the sky. Rain! It had rained for weeks, so that now even the smallest stream was a formidable torrent. As a result, how could they hope to cross the Vistula on their way to Duke Swientopelk's country? After so much rain, the great river must surely be impassable!

True enough. When the group finally reached the Vistula—at the town of Vishogrod, home of Duke Conrad of Masovia—they found that no boat-man would take them across. The swirling current was far too dangerous.

"But we can't afford to stay in Masovia!" exclaimed Hyacinth. "Surely there must be some-one here who will help us get on with our journey?"

The people of Vishogrod shook their heads.

Perhaps tomorrow the trip could be arranged, but certainly not today. Then they clustered around the four friars, their eyes wide with wonder. Never had they seen such a striking sight as that made by these black-and-white-clad preachers, who, vowed to poverty, had walked the one hundred and seventy miles from Cracow in the manner of the poorest peasant.

"Don't you have any home?" whispered one man unbelievingly.

"Sssh!" replied another. "Father Hyacinth just told us that his friars do have monasteries, but that most of the time they go about among the poor and preach."

After talking further with the people of Vishogrod, most of whom were pagans, Hyacinth realized that there was no use in trying to find a boat. "I guess we'll just have to ask Our Lady to help us across," he said. "Come, my sons. We mustn't delay any longer."

At once the curiosity of the people was aroused. *Our Lady?* Then a woman was going to help the strangers ford the raging river? But how could that be? Why, there wasn't a man in all Vishogrod who would attempt the perilous trip, let alone a lady!

As the onlookers questioned one another eagerly, Hyacinth and his friars set out for the river bank. About half a mile distant, on the opposite shore, was their destination, the imposing castle of Duke Conrad of Masovia.

"We can't possibly reach it," whispered Godinus to Florian. "Just look at those waves!"

Due to the recent heavy rains, the Vistula was now an angry gray mass, topped here and there with ominous whitecaps. It was easy to see why no boatman dared to make the journey across. And yet somehow Florian was hopeful. If Father Hyacinth had said that Our Lady would help them, she would do so. Perhaps even now she was inspiring some timid soul to offer his boat. In a few minutes. . .

Suddenly a startling sight met Florian's eyes, and he uttered a cry of dismay. Father Hyacinth, who had been kneeling in silent prayer by the river, had arisen, made the Sign of the Cross over the turbulent waters, and stepped off the bank! But even as Florian cried out, Hyacinth set foot firmly upon the waves, as though he were treading dry land! Soon he was several yards from the shore and headed for the Duke's castle on the other side of the river!

"Oh, no!" cried the young friar weakly. "I must be dreaming!"

But it was no dream. Benedict and Godinus were also witnessing the wonderful sight, and the citizens of Vishogrod as well. Every face was pale, every heart pounding with excitement. Not only was a man walking on the water before their very eyes! That water had suddenly become as calm as a mill-pond, marred only slightly by what appeared to be footprints!

"Father Hyacinth wants you to walk on the water, too!" cried a little girl suddenly. "Don't you see him beckoning to you?"

Yes—apparently Hyacinth was surprised that his

young disciples had not been following him. Now
he was standing in mid-stream and beckoning
vigorously. But although they were accustomed to
obey their Father Prior in all things, this time it
was different. The three young friars could not
move even one inch toward the river. It was as
though all power had departed from their limbs.
For the time being they could only stare at the solitary black-and-white-clad figure standing far out on
the water—stare and tremble.

Finally Hyacinth took pity on his young friends.
He returned to the bank and gave them an
encouraging smile. "Is this the way to show your
gratitude for Our Lady's help?" he chided gently.
"Come, if you're too tired to walk across the river,
we'll make the trip in an easier fashion."

Before his startled audience could catch its
breath, he had taken off his black cloak and spread
it carefully upon the water. "Don't be frightened,"
he said. "Just step on the cloak and see what
happens."

The three young men stared in amazement, then
slowly advanced to the river's edge. But it was with
great fear, for no one of them could believe that
when he stepped upon the cloak it would not sink.
Hesitantly Florian put one foot down. Wonder of
wonders! The cloth supported him! And it was dry!
An instant later Benedict and Godinus experienced
the same miracle. Far from turning into a limp and
sodden mass and sinking to the bottom, the cloak
continued to float, bearing the weight of all three.
Then Hyacinth made a sign, and the cloak began

to move swiftly and surely after him towards the other side of the river!

Naturally the people of Vishogrod were beside themselves. Who were these strangers? Surely the God they worshiped must be the True God!

"I'm going to get my boat and go after them!" cried a fisherman suddenly. "Who wants to come along?"

Instantly there was a mad scramble to fill this and other boats, and soon the now peaceful Vistula presented a busy scene. Almost half the population of Vishogrod was on its way across the river—all eyes fixed upon the four religious who continued to defy the laws of nature in so spectacular a fashion.

As might be expected, the miraculous crossing was witnessed by many from the opposite bank. When Hyacinth and his friars finally stepped ashore here, it was to be greeted by an eager and awe-struck throng, a few of whom had received the Christian Faith in years past but since had drifted away. Now they fell upon their knees to make a general Confession of their sins. Oh, how true that they had broken all the Commandments—even to the point of committing murder and worshiping false gods!

"Forgive us, Father!" they begged earnestly. "Give us your blessing, and we'll try not to sin anymore!"

"Yes, but don't leave Vishogrod!" implored the others, crowding around Hyacinth and clutching at his habit. "We'll build a fine monastery for you if

"DON'T BE FRIGHTENED," HE SAID.

you'll only stay and teach our children."

Hyacinth's heart sank as he listened to the eager pleading of these new friends. Of course he knew that Masovia, or northern Poland, was lacking in priests. But at least it was not a totally pagan country such as Prussia. Therefore, much as he would have liked to help the Masovians, he knew that his duty lay still farther to the North. He must push on to Pomerania, obtain the friendship of Duke Swientopelk, then build a convent that would not be too far away from the Prussian frontier. Later his friars would spread the True Faith in this wild and dangerous land.

Thus it was that only a brief stop was made at Vishogrod, and then the four apostles continued on their way. A week or so later they reached Pomerania and obtained an interview with Duke Swientopelk. Knowing that the latter was a blunt and hot-tempered man, they were pleasantly surprised at the cordial reception he gave them and at his generous response to their appeal for land.

"Of course you may have land," he announced readily, "and money for a new monastery, too. Have you any idea where you would like to build, Father Hyacinth? In some valley, perhaps? Or on a mountaintop?"

The friar pointed toward the sea. "If you could arrange it, Your Highness, I'd like to have the island of Gedan," he said hopefully.

The Duke stared in amazement. *Gedan?* But this was only a wilderness, a tiny uninhabited island a mile or so out in the Baltic! Surely Father Hyacinth was not much of a bargainer...to choose this remote and worthless piece of ground when he might have a whole valley for the asking...or a wooded mountain....

Hyacinth smiled as he read the Duke's thoughts, but he did not change his mind. Somehow he had a feeling that Gedan was one of the most valuable sections of Pomerania. Although it was isolated now, and a wilderness, there would come a day when the waters of the Baltic would complete a remarkable change. Even now tons of sand were being deposited by the tide in such a manner that gradually the channel between Gedan and the mainland was becoming very shallow. As a result, in a few years there would no longer be an island. On one side nature would have joined Gedan to the mainland, thus creating an excellent harbor.

"When this happens, Gedan will become a great center of commerce," Hyacinth told himself. "Boats will come here from all over the world. Some will continue to call the place Gedan, others Sdansk, but most people will know it by the name of Danzig. God willing, our friars will have some part in making Danzig a truly Christian city."

CHAPTER 10

THE LIGHT COMES TO RUSSIA

IN DUE course the island of Gedan was given to Hyacinth by Duke Swientopelk, and a temporary shelter erected there to serve as a convent. Soon the little establishment was dedicated to Saint Nicholas, and then Hyacinth made the announcement for which all had waited so long. Yes—it was time for him to leave Pomerania!

"For Prussia, Father?" asked Benedict eagerly. "Are you really going to preach in that wild country?"

Hyacinth's eyes were kind as he looked at Benedict. What a good young man this was! How eager to serve God, no matter what the cost!

"You seem to be very interested in Prussia, my son."

"Oh, yes—Father—especially now that I've seen something of this northern country and know how much there is to be done for souls."

Hyacinth smiled. "Well, you'll go to Prussia but not just yet. Can you guess why?"

Benedict shook his head. "No, Father. I haven't

the least idea."

"Well, you can't go to Prussia just yet because I'm making you Prior of this monastery in Gedan. Kneel down now, and I'll give you my blessing."

Scarcely knowing what he did, Benedict fell upon his knees. Surely Father Hyacinth didn't mean to entrust the new Monastery of Saint Nicholas to *him!* Yet before many hours had passed, he realized that this was exactly the case. Yes, while Hyacinth went off on fresh missionary journeys with Brothers Florian and Godinus, Benedict would remain in Gedan. In his hands would be the important task of recruiting friars for eventual missionary work among the Prussians.

Of course Hyacinth knew that when he appointed Benedict as Prior of Gedan he was giving him an enormous task—one far more difficult than any undertaken by Herman at Friesach or Henry at Olmütz. For though Pomerania was no longer a pagan land, the people there were far from being well-grounded in the Faith. It would be much harder to secure vocations to the religious life along the Baltic Sea than it had ever been in Austria or Moravia. Yet Hyacinth knew that miracles can be accomplished through prayer and sacrifice. Therefore his parting advice to Benedict would be this: to put himself at the complete disposal of the Heavenly Father—to do or to suffer in accordance with His Will. Every day he was to renew this offering. Then there would be no doubt that any work he might undertake would be blessed a hundredfold. And when he had taught other young men to make this consecration, what great good would result—for themselves and for every soul in the North!

It was a few days later that Hyacinth gave the new Prior a final blessing and his promise to return to Gedan within two years. Then with Florian and Godinus as companions, he prepared for a journey to Russia.

The two young friars were really excited at this, for since childhood they had known that Poland's eastern neighbor afforded a fertile missionary field. Yet, this was not because the country was truly pagan. Actually, Russia had been Christian since around the year 955.

"Today every city has its churches and monasteries," Hyacinth explained as they set out on their journey. "Yet there is work for us because for generations the Russian bishops and priests have been living in error. Like so many others in the East, particularly in Turkey and Greece, they accept only part of what the Church teaches. And since the clergy are in error, so, naturally, are the people. They have been led astray so completely that they no longer understand what is meant by Truth."

"I know about one of the errors in Russia," said Florian. "The priests and people don't recognize the Pope as the Vicar of Christ on earth. Isn't that so, Father?"

Hyacinth nodded. "That is one of the errors. But there are several others. For instance, the Russian Christians don't believe that in Purgatory souls are cleansed from the stain of sin or that the bread and wine are changed into the Body and Blood of Christ at the very instant the priest pronounces the words of Consecration. They say, too, that the Holy Ghost proceeds from God the Father alone and not also from the Son."

For a moment the two young religious were silent. Then Godinus looked thoughtfully at his beloved superior. "In what city should we start to work for these poor people, Father? Moscow, perhaps? or Smolensk?"

Hyacinth shook his head. Moscow and Smolensk were in northern Russia, almost in the same latitude as Gedan, but he had decided not to go there as yet. Rather, he and his young companions would strike out for the southeast—for the great city of Kiev, six hundred miles away.

"Kiev is the capital of Russia, my sons, the center of art and culture," he explained. "It will pay us to try and secure a foothold there."

During the next few weeks, Florian and Godinus learned many things from their Father Prior besides the fact that the Christian peoples of eastern Europe and western Asia denied the authority of the Pope. For instance, they glimpsed some of the great works accomplished in Bohemia by Father Ceslaus, Hyacinth's older brother. The two had not seen each other for more than seven years, but occasionally travelers from Prague arrived in Cracow with news of Ceslaus' apostolic labors.

"Ceslaus did wonders as Prior of Saint Clement's," said Hyacinth one morning. "Thank God for that!"

Godinus looked up quickly. "*Did*, Father? But surely nothing has happened to stop the good work!"

Hyacinth smiled. "Haven't I told you? Ceslaus is no longer in Prague. Last year he left the work in charge of Father Jerome and went to Breslau. These days he is preaching at the Cathedral by a special invitation from Bishop Lawrence."

So the three talked, with the young religious continuing to learn still more about Father Ceslaus. For instance, shortly after the latter's arrival in Prague in the year 1220, he had founded not only the Monastery of Saint Clement for his preaching friars but also a convent for nuns. Then his marvelous skill as a spiritual director was soon discovered, and many good souls placed themselves under his care. Now that he was established in Breslau, the same state of affairs prevailed. None other than Henry and Hedwig, the Duke and Duchess of Silesia, were his penitents.

"Of course you've heard of them?" asked Hyacinth.

Florian and Godinus nodded eagerly. Duke Henry was one of the more important men in northern Europe. As for the Duchess Hedwig, her fame had spread far and wide. She was a truly Christian wife and mother, and only on the Last Day would the full extent of her prayers and sacrifices for others be known.

The days rolled by, and Hyacinth and his companions pushed on toward Kiev. Whenever they passed through a town or village, they always stopped to preach. Generally their audiences were large ones, for even the most ignorant peasants were hungry for Truth. The lives of these peasants were extremely hard, since most of them were but slaves to the soil of their masters. Yet once they had heard Hyacinth speak of God and of Heaven, somehow things were changed. And why not? Look at the comforting message he brought! For instance: a poor and ignorant man is entitled to justice, even as his neighbor who has education and social position. Too seldom can he find it in this world, of course, and yet how wonderful when he does! But if justice to the downtrodden is a cause for joy when administered by human hands, how much more so when it comes from the hands of God! Then it is Perfect Justice and without end. Nothing can ever mar it or take it away.

"If I could believe this, no pain would be too hard to bear," said a young man to Brother Florian one day. "But how can I be sure that there really is a Heaven? That someday all injustice will be at an end?"

There were different ways of answering this question, but Florian chose the simplest. "Why, ask God to help you to believe," he said. "Ask the dead—including perhaps your dead friends and relations."

The young man stared. "*The dead?* But what can they do?"

"The dead, if they died in the grace of God, are in either Heaven or Purgatory now. They are, or at least will be, saints and supremely happy. Naturally they want you to be happy, too. If you ask them very humbly for the gift of faith, their prayers will obtain it for you. The main thing to remember is this: you must keep on asking. You must never give up, even when you feel that all the prayers in the world are useless."

There was something pathetic about the young stranger, and late that night Florian prayed for him with more than ordinary fervor. How true that faith in God exceeds all wealth or power, he reflected. A child may have this faith, or a hopeless cripple, and thus know a happiness that kings cannot buy or great scholars comprehend. And as he pondered on this fact, Florian redoubled his prayers for the young man he had met that morning and for all the other souls in this vast Northland who were hungry for God's Truth.

"Heavenly Father, let everybody in Poland receive and cherish the gift of the True Faith!" he prayed. "And someday let the whole country understand the complete meaning of the Cross—that it is an emblem not only of pain and humiliation but also of joy and victory!"

It was close to midnight when the young religious arose from his knees, his mind still busy with the thought that to most people the Cross is a reminder of Good Friday but hardly ever of Easter Sunday.

"No wonder we try to run away from it," he told himself. "Until Father Hyacinth explained things, I ran away, too. Now I understand the wonderful secret a little better: that when we accept the Cross readily, the suffering it brings becomes tinged with real joy. But when we complain about the Cross and try to escape it, our souls become slaves to fear and pain. Then life is nothing but an endless procession of unhappy hours."

As he went to join Hyacinth and Godinus for the recitation of Matins and Lauds, Florian suddenly realized that the midnight sky outside his window was alive with unearthly beauty. Mighty arcs of green, blue and white flame were mounting from the horizon in every direction, so that the slumbering countryside now stood out in bold relief.

"The northern lights!" he whispered in an awed voice. "When have I ever seen them so beautiful?"

Yes—the *aurora borealis*, that miracle of nature so common in northern regions, was suddenly possessed of a strange fascination for Florian. Before its gleaming radiance the shadows of night had fled, and now the whole outside world was transformed into a place of beauty.

"It's the same with Father Hyacinth's work," the young friar told Godinus the next morning. "For seven years he's been bringing the light of the True Faith into these dark and pagan lands and transforming the souls of men. Fathers Herman and Henry have been doing the same thing, too—in Austria and Moravia."

"Don't forget Father Ceslaus and his work in Prague and Breslau," put in Godinus. "He's also been a true light to many. And of course our own Brother Benedict will do much good in the far North."

Florian nodded. "And now it's our turn. *We go*

to Russia. Oh, my brother! I wonder if we'll really have success there?"

Yes, Vladimir Rurikovitch, the Grand Prince of Kiev, distrusted anyone who paid homage to Gregory the Ninth, the recent successor to Honorius the Third as Pope and Bishop of Rome. From childhood he had been taught to consider all true Catholics, whom he called "western Catholics," as heretics, and to consider his own people, mistakenly called "eastern Catholics," as possessors of the true faith. Hence his allegiance in spiritual matters was given to the Patriarch of Constantinople, not to Pope Gregory.

Because of this, Hyacinth had long ago prepared his young followers for the possibility of an unfriendly reception at Kiev—even for martyrdom. Therefore, when they glimpsed the city for the first time, all fell upon their knees and prayed for strength and courage. Only then did they think to look at the beauty of Kiev, how majestically it arose from the Dnieper river, terrace by terrace, to the dark and mysterious forests beyond. Yet even as they looked at the imposing Russian capital, the same conviction was growing in each heart. The golden domes of Kiev's four hundred churches, the slender minarets rising from the many monasteries, were symbols of error rather than invitations to rejoice at man's artistic skill.

"Come, we mustn't delay even one moment," Hyacinth said firmly. "There will be much hard missionary work here."

True enough. The three friars had real difficulty

in obtaining an interview with the Grand Prince Vladimir. When it did come, they found him firm in his refusal to allow them to preach in his city.

"But we only wish to speak of God!" said Hyacinth quickly. "Why should you object to that, Your Majesty, when you yourself are a Christian?"

Vladimir's eyes narrowed. "I object because you come from Rome, from the Pope," he said stiffly. "Here in Russia we want nothing to do with *him*. And forgive my speaking plainly, but I really cannot welcome you to Kiev, Reverend Fathers. I suggest that you go elsewhere to do your preaching—and at once!"

With this the Grand Prince got to his feet, gathered his royal robes about him, bowed, then turned and disappeared through a secret door behind his magnificent throne. Immediately six armed guards stepped forward to escort the friars back to the palace gates. But as the group went in endless procession from one richly carpeted room to the next, an eleven-year-old girl suddenly appeared in one of the doorways. She was dressed in pale blue velvet, with a small gold crown atop her dark hair. Apparently she was an important member of the royal household, for with one accord the six guards came to a flourishing halt before her and bowed to the ground.

At this sudden stop Florian and Godinus looked down at the little stranger. A real princess! And how beautiful! Yet Hyacinth sensed there was some defect in this child's beauty. Somehow his compassionate heart told him that she was not as other girls her age. Ah, no! The dark eyes lifted to his own held the vaguely empty look of one who has been blind since birth.

Suddenly Cracow's famous preacher advanced toward the young princess. A tender smile was on his lips as he laid his hand in blessing over the sightless eyes. "Receive what you most desire, child," he whispered, "in the Name of the Father, and of the Son, and of the Holy Ghost."

"RECEIVE WHAT YOU MOST DESIRE, CHILD,"
HE WHISPERED.

CHAPTER 11

GATHERING CLOUDS

IN JUST a few minutes the entire palace was in an uproar. Servants, guards—even the royal family itself—were running hither and yon, the same exciting words on every tongue. Little Princess Anna could see!

"I'm sure the new priest did it!" cried the child joyfully, pointing to Father Hyacinth. "I heard him praying over me, and now things aren't dark anymore."

Unashamed of the tears coursing down his cheeks, Vladimir pressed his little daughter to his heart. What joy! What marvelous and unexpected joy! But even as the happy tears flowed, the mind of the Grand Prince was troubled. How could he ever repay this Polish friar who had made all the happiness possible? Why, only a short while ago he had ordered him out of the palace, even out of Kiev!

"Father, forgive me!" he murmured humbly. "What reward will you have for the miracle?"

Hyacinth shook his head. "Reward? Why should I have a reward, Your Majesty? or gratitude? Don't

113

you know that God worked this wonder so that you would be brought closer to Him?"

Vladimir hesitated. "Yes, Father. But just the same, there must be something you would like. Can't you tell me what it is?"

Once again Hyacinth shook his head. He would claim no reward. As he continued to smile kindly upon the Russian monarch, the latter's pride suddenly crumbled. Could it be that this foreigner professed the True Faith, and not the clergy of Kiev? That the "western Catholics" were in the right, instead of those who paid homage to the Patriarch of Constantinople?

"Father!" he whispered hoarsely. "Something's happening to me! And I . . . I don't understand what it is!"

Quickly Hyacinth stretched out a reassuring hand. Well he knew what was happening. The Devil was making one last effort to keep Vladimir's soul in the darkness of heresy. But surely he wouldn't succeed! Three preaching friars stood ready to pay whatever price God's Justice deemed necessary. And behind them were others—the priests, lay Brothers and cloistered nuns in various parts of Europe who were fellow-members of the Order of Preachers. Vowed to God's service, they had made the saving of souls their life's work. There were the secular Tertiaries to help, too—the men and women living in the world who had affiliated themselves with the Order. Oh, there was a real army ready to assist Vladimir in his hour of need! At this very minute there were souls praying and suffering for him in Italy, France, Spain, Austria, Poland. . . .

As Vladimir continued to look beseechingly into Hyacinth's eyes, the fierce struggle within him subsided. A wonderful peace crept over him, and suddenly he fell upon his knees. "Father, I confess my error," he whispered. "From now on I will recognize Pope Gregory as Head of the True Church. I will do everything necessary to be counted as one of his loyal sons."

Hyacinth smiled. How mysterious the workings of grace! A short while ago Vladimir had been a proud and obstinate man. Now he was on his knees like the simplest peasant, begging for instructions in the spiritual life. But what would be the cost of this conversion? or that of even one more soul in Russia?

"God will tell us after a while," he thought. "There will be some new suffering—and of course the grace to bear it bravely."

A few days later the people of Kiev were amazed to discover that their Grand Prince was no longer a heretical "eastern Catholic" and that his family had also turned from Constantinople to Rome. But this amazement increased when they learned the chief reason for the surprising conversion: namely, that the little Princess Anna now enjoyed perfect vision because a "western Catholic" priest had placed his hands upon her and prayed.

"Who is this priest?" asked one man curiously.

"Yes, where did he come from?" put in another.

"He must be a saint, even if he is a 'western Catholic,'" added a third.

Soon an interesting story was being pieced
together. Father Hyacinth was a member of the
illustrious Polish family of Odrowatz. He had been
born in 1185 in the ancestral castle near Breslau,
capital of Silesia. He had a brother Ceslaus, one
year older than himself. Almost from babyhood the
two had shown an interest in spiritual matters, and
so ultimately their education was entrusted to a
priest-uncle, Ivo Odrowatz, canon of the Cathedral
in Cracow. This good man welcomed his nephews
to Poland, trained them in secular and religious
subjects, and finally sent them to the Universities
of Prague and Bologna for higher studies. Later he
was delighted to hear that they wanted to be
priests. So there were more studies, reception of
Holy Orders, and then Hyacinth and Ceslaus
became assistants to their uncle. In the year 1220,
when their uncle succeeded the saintly Vincent
Kadlubek as Bishop of Cracow, the two young
clerics accompanied him on a visit to Rome. Here
they met Dominic de Guzman, founder of the
Friars Preachers, and joined his Order. Ever since,
except for the time spent in a very brief novitiate,
they had been preaching to the peoples of Austria,
Moravia, Bohemia and Poland. A short while ago
Hyacinth had even made himself known in Pomerania, with the prospect of going into Prussia in the
near future.

"Why did he ever change his mind?" the Russian
monks asked one another nervously. "Why did he
come here to Kiev?"

There was no doubt about it. The local clergy

were really on edge over Hyacinth's presence in the city, especially since the Grand Prince made no secret of his admiration and was constantly in the friars' company. Why, he had even ordered that a fine monastery be built for them, and at royal expense! He had also given permission for them to preach to the people.

"No good will come of this," murmured the Russian priests enviously. "Wait and see if there's not trouble in Kiev—and very soon."

As the days passed, Hyacinth realized that he and his young companions were actually hated by the leaders of the "eastern Catholics." If it were not that the soldiers of the Grand Prince followed them wherever they went, their very lives would be in danger.

"The Russian priests are dreadfully jealous, Father," reported Florian one morning. "They can't forget that God allowed you to cure the little princess and so win the patronage of the Grand Prince. And of course now that we have a fine new monastery. . ."

Godinus nodded. "That's a real blow to their pride. And can you imagine their feelings if we should ever secure any vocations to the religious life? That would surely be the last straw, wouldn't it, Father?"

Hyacinth smiled. "Possibly, my son. And yet that is just what is going to happen. Within two years we'll clothe several young men in the habit of our Order. More than that. A number of Russian priests will also be converted and come to live in this new monastery."

Godinus and Florian looked wide-eyed at each other. This was almost too much to believe—that some of Kiev's heretical priests should acknowledge their error, lay aside important positions, then ask for the lowest place in a monastery of "western" friars!

"It will happen thus within two years," repeated Hyacinth firmly. "However, we won't think about it now. We won't even try to do very much about converting the 'eastern Catholics' or their leaders. Rather, we shall devote ourselves to another group of people. Who are they, Brother Florian?"

"The pagans," replied the latter quickly. "There are many of them in the city."

It was true. Christianity in a heretical form had made much headway in Russia, yet there were still thousands of men and women who worshiped idols. Regularly they came together for their heathenish rites, offering sacrifices to statues of iron and stone. Usually they congregated in remote places, and when Hyacinth learned that one of their favorite haunts was a wooded island in the Dnieper, not far from Kiev, he determined to go there. God willing, he would bring something of the True Faith to these benighted souls.

Very early one morning he set out on his mission. At first he had thought to go alone, and told Florian and Godinus to spend the time of his absence in prayer before the Blessed Sacrament. But at the last moment he had a change of heart. Yes, he would take a companion. Brother Martin, who had arrived only recently from the monastery at Sandomierz, might come with him. On the walk to the river bank he could make a report of all that had happened in Poland since Hyacinth's departure over six months ago.

The younger religious tried not to question the command, although on his arrival from Sandomierz last week he had made a complete report on affairs at home.

"Real trouble is brewing in Poland, Father," he began earnestly. "Leszek of Cracow has been killed by Duke Swientopelk of Pomerania. His widow, Grzymyslava, and their little son have taken refuge in Breslau with Duke Henry and the Duchess Hedwig. The throne is empty, and it looks like war between Swientopelk, Henry and Duke Conrad of Masovia."

"Conrad? But why should he fight one who gives refuge to his brother's widow and child?"

"It is because of Duke Conrad that Grzymyslava and her two-year-old Boleslaus have gone to Breslau, Father. You see, Conrad wants the throne of Cracow for himself."

Hyacinth sighed as he murmured a prayer for Duke Leszek, his old friend and patron. War was a dreadful matter, even when waged in a just cause. But a civil war, inspired by petty jealousies within a country's borders...by greedy men who would kill their own flesh and blood in order to obtain more power...

"We need saints to atone for such evil!" he thought. "Holy women like Duchess Hedwig and heroic men like Bishop Stanislaus! Perhaps then

God's Justice would be appeased and there would be peace and unity in Poland."

For several minutes Martin was silent, aware that Hyacinth's thoughts were far away. Then suddenly the latter returned to himself. "Tell me more," he urged. "What about the Prussians? Has Brother Benedict been able to do anything for them?"

At once Martin began to describe the troubled conditions in the far North. No, the little community at Gedan had too few members for missionary work. Yet steps had been taken to subdue, if not to convert, the warlike Prussians. Duke Conrad of Masovia, who had invaded Silesia in pursuit of Grzymyslava and her infant son, was also active along the Baltic. Recently he had asked the Knights of the Cross to come into his territory and undertake a crusade into Prussia. Herman von Salza, leader of the Knights (who were of German birth and soldiers as well as religious), had agreed. He and his followers would fortify the more important towns in Masovia and devote themselves to establishing law and order in the North.

"There are some who question this step," said Brother Martin. "They say it's folly to invite any Germans into Poland, even for religious reasons. They think there are ambitious men among the Knights of the Cross who will insist on ruling Prussia once the pagans are crushed. Why, a few even believe that Prussia will become a German province some day—and all because of Duke Conrad's action!"

Hyacinth did not answer, nor did he ask for

further news of his homeland. Instead, he strode
silently toward the outskirts of the city, his eyes
lowered, his lips moving in prayer. Only after half
an hour's brisk walk did he seem to remember that
he had a companion. Then he came to a halt,
tapped Brother Martin lightly on the shoulder and
pointed straight ahead. "There's the river, my son.
And the island where the heathen gather."

Martin looked up. They had finally reached the
outskirts of Kiev and now were standing on a grassy
hillside overlooking the majestic Dnieper. It was a
few minutes after sunrise, and splashes of purple,
crimson and gold lay reflected in the tranquil water
like so many gorgeous banners. Reflected also were
the thickly set pine trees of the little island in
mid-stream.

"It's beautiful!" murmured Martin, carried out of
himself at the peaceful scene. "Oh, thank you for
bringing me, Father!"

For a moment all was silence as Hyacinth fixed
his eyes in careful scrutiny upon the island. Then
suddenly his hands clenched. Drawn up at one side
of the island were several small boats. And toward
the center, from amidst the thick trees, rose a slender column of smoke!

"The pagans!" he whispered. "They're offering
sacrifice!"

Yes, the hour of sunrise was a favorite time for
idol worship and gratefully Hyacinth realized that
his plans were working out well. More than a hundred men and women must be on the island, kneeling in a secret grove before the ugly statue they

believed to be a god. Already there must have been prayers and hymns, then the burning of a lamb or calf before the idol. Soon the service would be over and the pagans would stream down to the their boats to return to their homes in Kiev.

"I've no time to lose," he said firmly. "Kneel down, Brother Martin, and pray that I do something really worthwhile to help these poor people!"

Before the young religious could realize what was happening, Hyacinth had turned and started down the grassy slope to the river's edge. His black cloak floated out behind him like a sail, and for a moment Martin knelt as one in a dream—forgetful of the command to pray. With what speed his beloved superior moved! Why, he was all but flying down the hill! Then the young friar grew really weak, for suddenly he understood that he was witnessing a genuine wonder. By now Father Hyacinth had reached the Dnieper and was starting to cross over to the island. But not in a boat. Ah, no! *Father Hyacinth was walking on the water as though it were dry land!*

"Mother of God!" cried Martin. "I heard that he did such a thing at Vishogrod. . .on the Vistula! But here? Before me? Oh, no! It's too much!"

Presently Hyacinth landed safely on the island, then disappeared into the thick woods. And, though Martin strained his eyes for several minutes, he could see him no longer. Nor was any sound to be heard save the harsh cries of the water birds as they circled over the river in search of food.

As he looked and listened in an agony of

HYACINTH WAS DRIVING BEFORE HIM
A HORRIBLE CREATURE!

suspense, the young religious tried to clasp his trembling hands in prayer. Oh, what was going to happen? Would Father Hyacinth really seek out the pagans? Would he put a stop to their heathen sacrifice?

"It can mean death," he thought. "Even I know that the Russian pagans are little more than crude barbarians."

Suddenly there was a clamor in the distance, muted at first, then growing louder, and with a sinking heart the young man realized that the pagans were aroused. They were pouring out of the woods with screams and shouts. But soon he could see that they were not attacking Father Hyacinth. They were not even making for the boats. Rather, they were throwing themselves on their knees in a very frenzy of terror. And why? Because a black-and-white-clad friar was striding out of the woods and driving before him a horrible creature—half man, half beast—with flames shooting from its mouth and eyes!

Martin's blood ran cold as he looked at the terrible sight. Could it be that this was the Devil? that Father Hyacinth's prayers had forced him to leave the idol and appear before the pagans in one of his hellish shapes?

"Oh, if only some of the Russian priests could be here!" whispered the young friar, his teeth chattering. "Maybe this would teach them not to speak ill of a true servant of God!"

CHAPTER 12

THE PASSING YEARS

MARTIN WAS wrong. When word of the miracle was noised about in Kiev, the jealousy of the heretical priests reached alarming proportions. So Father Hyacinth had gone to the island and found the pagans worshiping before an old oak tree? With one blow he had sent the great tree crumbling into dust? As the Evil One emerged from the tree, he had fought with him hand to hand, then thrown him into the Dnieper?

"Nonsense!" cried one of the Russian priests as the exciting story was repeated for still another time. "This is nothing but a stupid western trick!"

"Yes," a companion hastened to add. "Father Hyacinth has always used underhanded means to gain power over the people."

"Why do we stand for it?" asked a third, who was a nephew of Kiev's Archbishop and therefore possessed of considerable authority. "If there are any more of these so-called miracles, why don't we complain to the Grand Prince and ask him to send this meddling westerner back to his own country?"

Much as the others hated Hyacinth, they were doubtful that such a plan would work. "The Grand Prince is very fond of the western friar," they said. "He'd never send him away—especially since he cured the little princess."

The Archbishop's nephew smiled grimly. "There are ways of dealing with all men," he observed, "even with a Grand Prince. Wait and see."

Hyacinth continued his work for souls in Kiev, curing the sick, converting sinners, training his young religious to be worthy servants of God. Then one day Vladimir Rurikovitch came to the monastery he had built for the Friars Preachers. His face was haggard, his step slow. In the two years since Hyacinth's arrival, this was the first time he had ever been unhappy at the thought of a visit with him.

"Don't feel too bad, Your Majesty," said Hyacinth kindly. "I think I know the whole story. Things have now come to this stage: unless I leave Kiev, you are in danger of losing the throne. Isn't that so?"

Vladimir's eyes were full of misery. "Yes, Father. The Russian priests have much political power, and they are angry that I have protected you so long. Lately they have threatened to depose me. Oh, what am I going to do? You're my friend, and I don't want you to go away! Yet the priests are in dead earnest..."

Hyacinth did his best to comfort the Grand Prince, for long ago he had foreseen the present situation and knew what he would do. Yes, even if the Russian clergy could be brought to think well of him, he would never stay permanently in Kiev.

After all, wasn't he a missionary? Hadn't it always been his plan to lay the foundations of a new community, then place it in charge of a younger friar and move on to fresh fields? He had done this in Friesach, Olmütz, Cracow, Sandomierz, Troppau, Gedan. Now he would repeat the process in Kiev. Brother Godinus would make an excellent Prior, and Brother Martin could help him.

"Surely the Russian clergy won't object if I leave these two young friars here, Your Majesty?"

Vladimir shook his head. "No, Father. It's you they hate. I'm sure they'll not make too much trouble for Brothers Martin or Godinus. After all, have *they* cured anyone of blindness? or walked dry-shod across the Dnieper? or wrestled with demons?"

Late that night Hyacinth knelt in the chapel before a statue of Our Lady. It was a beautifully carved piece of alabaster, weighing about fifty-five pounds, a gift from the Grand Prince to Hyacinth and his community. In the light of the flickering candles the delicate features seemed to take on life, and suddenly the friar hid his face in his hands. An artist had made of this alabaster an inspiring and lovely thing, and yet it was as nothing to Our Lady's true beauty.

"Dearest Mother, through God's grace I have seen you many times," he thought. "And yet even now I don't know what you are really like. You have always had to keep your total beauty hidden from me. But in Heaven! Oh, how different things will be then! When may I go there, Mother? When may I see you face to face?"

Even as he prayed, Hyacinth felt that as yet God did not will him to rest from his labors. He was but forty-four years old, and there was so much to be done in the Northland! Prussia was wild and uncivilized, Poland split by civil war, Russia infected with heresy, both western and eastern Asia overrun with the barbarian Tartars. Oh, there were millions and millions of souls waiting to be told about God and Heaven!

"Please help me to do something for them!" he whispered, gazing up suddenly into Our Lady's face. "Oh, Mother! Never leave me on my travels!"

A few days later Hyacinth installed Godinus as Prior of the monastery in Kiev, gave the little community his blessing, said farewell to the Grand Prince and his family, then set out with Florian for Cracow, some five hundred miles to the west. As usual, the two friars preached in the villages and towns that lay along their route, and in eastern Galicia they met with real success. The city of Lemberg offered them land and funds for a monastery.

Hyacinth was delighted. "When we reach Cracow, we can send Father Gerard to look after details," he informed Florian. "Oh, how pleased Uncle Ivo will be!"

But when the two finally reached Cracow, bad news awaited them. Bishop Ivo was dead! He had passed away on a recent journey to Rome. More than that. The Friars Preachers in Poland now possessed a martyr in their ranks. Father Beranger, who had been appointed to succeed Ivo as Bishop, was also dead. He had lost his life at the hands of the pagans in Dalmatia, even before he could be consecrated a Bishop.

"The good soul was very young to die," Hyacinth thought, his heart torn with grief at the distressing news. "Why, it seems only yesterday that I gave Beranger the habit, helped him in his studies for the priesthood, even arranged that he preach among the Dalmatians!"

But as he thought upon the untimely passing of this cherished disciple, a mysterious joy crept into Hyacinth's heart. If God willed that good works should prosper when watered with the tears of sacrifice, how much more so when they sprang from sacrifice in its most complete form: *martyrdom of soul or body!* From now on, because of Father Beranger's holy death, surely the work of the Friars Preachers would be blessed with true success—in Poland and throughout the entire Northland!

"Lord, if it be Your Holy Will, let me be a martyr, too!" Hyacinth often prayed. *"Please!"*

As the years passed, this hope of dying in the cause of Truth remained firmly fixed in Hyacinth's mind. He carried it with him as he and his friars worked for souls in the far North, journeying along the shores of the Baltic and even westward to Denmark, Sweden and Norway. It was with him as he accompanied the Knights of the Cross in their crusades against the Prussians, as he founded his monasteries of preaching friars at Plock and Poznan and in the Silesian towns of Oppeln, Liegnitz, Schweidnitz, Glogau, Brieg and Oels. And then one day martyrdom was no longer something impossible or remote. In the year 1236, when Father Jordan of Saxony called for a General Chapter of the Order in Paris, the Christians of western Europe realized there was every chance that they might be martyrs, too—and within a very short time.

"The Tartars are ready to sweep over the whole of Europe!" warned Bela the Fourth, King of Hungary. "Batu Khan is out to conquer the world!"

Batu Khan! This was a name to send fear throughout Christendom, for it belonged to the grandson of the ruthless Genghis Khan—the Tartar chieftain who some years ago had led his barbarian hordes in powerful sweeps across China and Turkestan, then mysteriously halted his westward march on the plains of the Crimea. He had died in 1227, and ever since, his armies had been peacefully encamped near the Black Sea. But if King Bela was right—if the Tartars were growing weary of the quiet life and Batu Khan was about to invade Europe. . .

"Russia will certainly be the first to suffer," Hyacinth told himself. "The Tartars will destroy everything there before they move to the West. Oh, my poor children in Kiev! What will become of you?"

Throughout the long journey to the General Chapter in Paris, Hyacinth often discussed the problem with his companions—Father Gerard, Prior to the monastery in Cracow, and Father Martin, successor to Godinus as Prior in Kiev.

"Yes, the Tartars will burn and destroy everything," Father Martin admitted readily. "And not only in Kiev. In Sandomierz and Cracow as well."

"*Cracow?* But surely they'll never reach there!" cried Father Gerard unbelievingly. "Why, we have thousands of strong young men in Poland who would die a hundred deaths before they allowed a Tartar to invade our country, to desecrate our churches, to carry off the women and children into slavery. . ."

"You forget one thing," interrupted Father Martin. "These days Poland has no real leader. Conrad of Masovia fights Henry of Silesia. Swientopelk of Pomerania, supposedly a Christian, incites the pagan Prussians to rise against the Knights of the Cross. Oh, we are so divided among ourselves—and for stupid reasons—that it will be almost impossible to unite against a common enemy! Isn't that true, Father Hyacinth?"

After a moment's hesitation the latter nodded slowly. "Yes, my son. But things are not quite as hopeless as they seem. Poland may be at odds with herself now; yet she will arise when the danger comes. She will stop the Tartars—and so completely that never again will Europe be threatened by them!"

At the stirring and prophetic tones in their superior's voice, Fathers Martin and Gerard looked at each other in awe. But even as they thrilled to the knowledge that their Father Hyacinth was a saint, that just now God must have given him still one more glimpse into the future, their hearts grew heavy. For the first time they noticed streaks of gray running through Hyacinth's hair. There were also faint lines about the eyes and mouth that had not been there at the beginning of the long trip to Paris.

Reading their thoughts, Hyacinth smiled. "Yes, I'm fifty-one years old, my sons—the age when our Father Dominic went to his reward."

"Oh, but say you'll be with us for a long time yet, Father!" pleaded Gerard.

"Yes," added Martin quickly. "Surely you wouldn't have us face the Tartars alone?"

For a long time Hyacinth was silent. Then he sighed and looked earnestly into the eyes of his companions. "My sons, the Heavenly Father has given me twenty-one more years in which to serve Him," he whispered softly. "Oh, pray that I use these years well! They will be such important ones for our work in Poland!"

Twenty-one more years! Fathers Martin and Gerard did not forget this. In fact, they passed it along wherever they traveled, so that finally there was not a monastery of the Order in Poland that did not know that Father Hyacinth would live to be seventy-two years of age. Despite the endless hardships he had taken upon himself for the salvation of souls, God would not call him to his reward until the year 1257.

This reassuring knowledge brought joy to Ceslaus, who had almost given up hope of ever meeting his brother again. It seemed so long since that day in 1220 when they had said farewell to each other in Friesach! And yet if Hyacinth was to live to be seventy-two years of age. . .

"Surely once in that time he will be able to come to Breslau," Ceslaus thought. "Or perhaps I could go to Cracow. It would do me good to visit my old home again."

Yet the months passed and no such opportunity arose. Since 1232 Ceslaus had been acting as Provincial of the Order in Poland and was very busy in and about Breslau. Somehow he had never found the chance to journey eastwards to Cracow. For that matter, Hyacinth was no longer at the Monastery of the Holy Trinity. By a strange turn of events, he had returned to Russia. The brethren in Kiev had elected him Prior, and it seemed that the hostility on the part of the heretical clergy had now largely died away.

One day in the year 1237 a number of friars in Breslau suggested to Ceslaus that he call a Provincial Chapter or meeting of the Priors under his control.

"The General Chapter in Paris last year dealt with matters relating to the whole Order, Father. Now we need a similar meeting, but on a smaller scale and devoted solely to the work in Poland. Don't you agree?"

Ceslaus did agree, and accordingly arranged for a Provincial Chapter to be held at Sandomierz in August, 1238—and with a happy heart, for at last here was the long-awaited chance to see Hyacinth. Since the latter was a Prior, he would have to attend the Chapter, make a complete report on the work being done for souls in and around Kiev, and outline his plans for the future.

Ceslaus reached the Monastery of Saint James in Sandomierz considerably ahead of the date scheduled for the Chapter. Indeed, it was only June of 1238, and therefore he was not surprised to find that the various Priors had not yet arrived.

"But we've had word, and they are on their way," Father Sadoc told the newcomer. "Oh, Father Ceslaus! How exciting for us to be hosts to so many adventurous priests! I can hardly wait to see Father Hyacinth! Such tales as I've heard about *him!*"

Ceslaus smiled at the speaker's enthusiasm. Yet even as he agreed that the approaching Chapter promised to produce many good results, and that it would be an excellent thing for the novices of Sandomierz to meet those friars who had established the Order in Poland, he was somewhat puzzled by the carefree and almost childlike attitude of Father Sadoc. Why, he must be a man in his late thirties, and yet he acted as though the Chapter would be something like a party! A party at which one would meet his best friends and have a thoroughly enjoyable time!

"Suppose you tell me a little about yourself, Father," Ceslaus suggested presently. "Have you been long in Sandomierz?"

Father Sadoc was delighted at this unexpected chance to walk and talk with the newly arrived Provincial, and in just a few minutes had described his early days in the Order. Despite his youthful manners, he was really a seasoned missionary. Eighteen years ago he had received the habit in Rome, and from no less a person than Father

Dominic. After the General Chapter in Bologna in 1221, he had been sent with three companions to preach in Hungary, particularly in the territories bordering along the Danube where lived many savage tribes.

"Oh, it was a fine life, Father, with plenty of hard work and exciting adventures! Why, do you know that once I even saw the Devil?"

"You saw the Devil, you say?"

"Yes, Father. I had been in Hungary just a short time. Then one night I awoke, and there was the Evil One right beside me. He had several wicked spirits with him, too. They were all in a great rage—screaming, cursing, even weeping bitter tears as they looked at my companions and me."

"But why, do you think?"

Sadoc smiled happily. "Because they knew that we would save many souls from Hell. They even said so. 'Look at these missionaries!' they cried. 'Why, they're mere boys! And to think that we have to be conquered by *them!*'"

For a moment all was quiet, and then Sadoc glanced hopefully at Ceslaus. "Oh, Father! What an amazing night that was for me! Do you suppose anything so wonderful will ever happen again?"

FATHER SADOC WAS DELIGHTED TO WALK AND
TALK WITH THE NEWLY ARRIVED PROVINCIAL.

CHAPTER 13

THUNDER IN THE EAST

GOD DID not will that Ceslaus should see into the future at this particular moment. Therefore, the question brought only a smile and the suggestion that Sadoc continue with his description of life in Hungary. But if he could have realized the truth, how overpowered Ceslaus would have been! For something truly wonderful was in store for Sadoc. Yes—in the year 1260 he would suffer a martyr's death at the hands of the barbarian Tartars! He would be Prior at Sandomierz then, and would gain his glorious crown in company with the forty-eight members of his community. The cruel martyrdoms would take place at Compline, while the brethren were singing the *Salve Regina*. And since this beautiful hymn was the death song of souls who went straight to Heaven in Our Lady's care, the custom would eventually arise in the Order of singing it at the bedside of every dying religious.

Nor would Sadoc and his brethren go to their deaths unprepared. Several hours before, after chanting Lauds in the chapel, they would learn of their approaching martyrdoms by miraculous means. The fact would be written in golden letters in the Martyrology, the large book from which the feast of the day is announced. Thus, Sadoc and his companions would have the extraordinary privilege of commemorating their holy deaths in the Psalms and prayers of the Divine Office—and this while they still lived!

God's Providence kept such wonders from Ceslaus, however, and so he continued to think of Sadoc as a most cheerful but otherwise rather average religious. His complete admiration was reserved for Hyacinth, whose arrival at Sandomierz for the Chapter was preceded by happy news.

"Last month our Father was staying near Cracow," explained the messenger who brought the good tidings. "A noble lady invited him to spend the Feast of Saint Margaret at her country estate and to preach to her servants and farm helpers."

"Of course he agreed?" broke in the Prior, for like everyone else at Sandomierz he had heard of Hyacinth's unusual kindness.

The messenger nodded. "Oh, yes, Father. And everyone was happy. First, because a saint was going to be with them. Second, because the fields gave promise of a splendid harvest. Why, never before had there been such wonderful acres of wheat and corn!"

"Then something dreadful happened?"

The messenger's voice took on solemn tones. "The day before Saint Margaret's feast there was a bad hailstorm. The wheat and corn were beaten flat to the ground. Everyone was in despair, particularly the peasants. How could they keep alive during the winter if there was no grain to make flour for bread?"

A ripple of excitement ran around the community. Had Father Hyacinth come to the rescue? Of course! But when? And how?

"The good man was as sad as anyone else," continued the messenger. "That night he told everyone in the neighborhood to pray. They were to ask God, as a child would ask its father, to help them in their great need. As for himself, he went to the village church and remained there all night. Those who crept in to watch him from time to time were moved to tears. It was worth any number of sermons just to see how he knelt before the Tabernacle, his arms outstretched, his face radiating love and confidence."

"Yes, but what happened?"

"*What happened?* Why, in the morning everything was all right! The flattened wheat and corn were as firm and upright as they had been before the storm. Truly, the Feast of Saint Margaret was never celebrated with such joy as it was on that country estate under Father Hyacinth's direction."

Thus another miracle was added to those already credited to Hyacinth's prayers. Yet, when he arrived at Sandomierz, he would only smile when asked about it. If he spoke of the great day at all, it was merely in connection with Margaret of Antioch, the virgin and martyr of the third century whom the

Church remembers each year on the twentieth day of July.

"The little saint will help us if we pray to her," he said gently. "Let's always remember that."

In due course the various Priors arrived at San- domierz and the business of the Provincial Chapter got underway. Each morning the friars assembled for the Holy Sacrifice, offered by Ceslaus. Then after reciting a portion of the Divine Office, they repaired to the Chapter Hall to discuss ways and means for extending the work of the Order.

"Wouldn't Lithuania be a good missionary field?" someone asked one day.

"Yes, and Latvia," put in another.

"What about Finland?" suggested a third voice.

Hyacinth got to his feet and faced his fellow- religious. "I was hoping to go to Lithuania in a year or two," he said. "The city of Vilna is growing rapidly these days. But somehow I think there will have to be a delay. . ."

A strained quality in the speaker's voice caused the assembled friars to look up in concern. Why should there be a delay in opening up the vast Northland to the True Faith? Yet, even as each asked himself this question, Hyacinth explained what he meant. At present he was Prior of Kiev, with two more years to serve. God willing, he would hasten to Lithuania and Latvia immediately at the close of his term. But surely everyone present real- ized that Poland was facing dire times? that possibly it was better to strengthen the faith of the people at home, particularly with regard to prayer and sacrifice, than to branch out into new fields?

"You mean we ought to do something about the Tartars, Father?" asked the Prior of Poznan.

"That's what I mean," said Hyacinth. And then he began to speak at great length about the Tartars, those fierce warriors who belonged to the yellow race and whose real homes were thousands of miles away in Asia. They were short men, with slanting eyes and long black hair, who for generations had roamed through China and neighboring lands, subduing weaker tribes by fire and sword. Probably no other creatures were so ruthless in warfare as the Tartars. They seemed to glory in bloodshed, and it would be hard to tell which was the worse fate: to be a man and to die at their hands in battle or by torture, or to be a woman condemned to follow the Tartar armies as a slave and beast of burden.

"They also make slaves of captured children," continued Hyacinth. "As for religion—ah, their only god is the 'god of war'!"

It was a gloomy picture that Hyacinth painted, enlivened by only one ray of hope. Yes, the Tartars were about to invade Europe. There would be wholesale massacres in villages and towns. Churches and monasteries, built at such great effort by the Cistercians, the Friars Preachers and other religious groups, would be completely destroyed. Yet the barbarians would be stopped in their dreadful march toward western Europe. A nation of brave people, held together not so much by political leadership as by a sublime faith in God, would stand in the way.

"Poland will be that nation!" declared Hyacinth triumphantly. "Because of the supreme sacrifice of her sons and daughters, Europe will be saved. Oh, my children! Do everything possible to prepare our people for their part! It will be so tragic, yet so glorious!"

When the Chapter was over, Ceslaus came to Hyacinth's cell. Humanly speaking, his heart was heavy. Something told him that this was the last time he would ever speak with his beloved brother. This in itself was sufficient cause for sadness, yet added to it was the dreadful realization that the Tartars were coming and that hundreds of churches and monasteries in Poland were doomed to destruction.

"It took so many years to build them!" he murmured. "Oh, Hyacinth! Why should all our hard work have to be destroyed now?"

For a moment the younger friar was silent as a familiar Polish legend flashed through his mind. Since childhood it had been a favorite with him, although he had not thought of it in a long time. Now, however. . .

"Let's talk about our country's first martyr," he suggested cheerfully.

Ceslaus looked up in genuine surprise. "*Bishop Stanislaus?* But why should we talk about him?"

"Because his story may help both of us. And if we use it in our sermons, it may help others, too."

So presently Hyacinth began to relate the familiar tale. Back in 1079, King Boleslaus the Second killed the Bishop while the latter was celebrating Mass. Then, fearing that the body might be venerated as that of a martyr, he gave orders that it should be cut in small pieces and the limbs thrown into a field.

Suddenly Ceslaus realized why Hyacinth was repeating the famous story. For generations the Polish people had seen a parallel between this dismemberment of the Bishop's body and the wars that ravaged their country and kept it from political unity. They believed that these trials were in punishment for the dreadful crime committed by Boleslaus the Second and that only after many years would full atonement be made and peace restored.

Reading his brother's thoughts, Hyacinth smiled. "You know the rest of the tale," he said. "Don't you agree that it should be stressed these days?"

Ceslaus was thoughtful. "Yes, but particularly the happy ending—how the canons of the Cathedral collected all the pieces of the body in the dead of night; how they put them together as well as they could, then hid them in a secret place..."

"And then, before they could arrange for burial, the pieces joined together and the Bishop's body was without the least scar or blemish?"

"That's right. Oh, Hyacinth! This *is* a wonderful story!" Hyacinth nodded. "Yes. And I really believe that what we were taught as children will come true: that someday Poland's scars will be healed and she will emerge from her years of suffering, victorious and united."

Comforted, the two brothers presently said farewell, and with far more joy than either had thought possible, for now it was as if they saw beyond the trials and bloodshed soon to be visited upon their beloved country. Yes, a cross was in the skies over Poland, but there was also a crown. And just as God had healed the wounds of Bishop Stanislaus, so in the end would He heal the wounds of the Bishop's nation—lovingly, completely.

Soon Hyacinth was on his way back to Kiev accompanied by the faithful Brother Florian. When the two finally glimpsed the city that had been home to them in recent years, the younger friar turned hopefully toward his superior.

"Kiev is so beautiful, Father! Isn't it possible that the Tartars may spare it from destruction?"

Hyacinth was silent for a moment, his eyes taking in the gorgeous panorama of golden domes and minarets. Yes, this capital of Russia was a rich prize, and possibly the barbarians might try to take it intact. Yet who in Kiev would be foolish enough to bargain with the Tartars? Even if it meant a temporary truce, there could be no real security for anyone paying tribute to Batu's heathen hordes.

"I don't think Kiev will be spared," he said finally. "In the end it will suffer the same fate as our Polish cities."

In early autumn of the year 1240 an army under Mangu Khan, cousin of the famed Batu, arrived at the Dnieper. As Florian had suggested, the Tartars were astounded at Kiev's beauty and at first attempted to take it without force. They camped quietly on the opposite bank of the river, then sent envoys with offers of peace. If the Russians would hand over the city, they said, there would be no loss of life or destruction of property. All that would be required was a reasonable tax to be paid by each person living within the walls. In return for this, the Tartars would protect Kiev against all enemies.

The Russians were not deceived by the seemingly generous terms. Who could trust the Tartars? They had tricked too many others in the past.

"We'll pretend we're interested, though," they told one another. "We'll play for time and try to outwit the enemy."

So while the envoys fretted and fumed, the Russians held their consultations. But everyone knew the truth. The delay was being used to build up the city's defenses. Once winter came and the Dnieper froze, it would be too late for this. Then the Tartar hordes could assemble on the thick ice and attack the city at many points.

As autumn passed, Hyacinth and his community made ready by prayer and sacrifice for the approaching storm. The Prior's heart was frequently heavy, for his term as superior was drawing to a close and this meant that soon he would have to leave Kiev whether the Tartars struck or not. Of course Godinus would make an able Prior, but what a hardship to leave this cherished son to the mercies of the barbarians! And the other friars as well!

"Go back to Poland while there's still time, Father!" begged the younger religious one day. "You may be killed if you stay here."

Hyacinth smiled, remembering those days when Godinus had set out with him on his first missionary journey to the North. How fearful the boy had been in the swamps and forests of Masovia! When crossing the Vistula on Hyacinth's cape! On the first interview with Duke Swientopelk! Yet now, because the Holy Ghost had answered his repeated requests for the Gift of Fortitude. . .

"You forget I am only fifty-five years old, my son," he said gently, "and apparently not to be blessed with martyrdom. No, I shall stay in Kiev until the storm breaks. Then God will tell me what to do."

It was on a morning in mid-November in the year 1240 that a terrified novice burst into the chapel where Hyacinth was just completing the Holy Sacrifice of the Mass.

"The Tartars, Father! They've come!"

Immediately a shiver ran through the community and all eyes turned upon the pale-faced novice. Surely the boy must be mistaken? So far the winter had been a mild one, and as yet the Dnieper was not frozen. Then how could the Tartars have arrived to attack the city? Yet even as each friar asked himself these questions, there was a succession of blood-curdling screams in the distance.

"They're coming!" cried the novice again, rushing toward the altar where Hyacinth was now reading the Last Gospel. "Oh, Father! What are we going to do?"

Hyacinth smiled encouragingly at the novice but continued with the words of Saint John. Only when he had closed the Missal and remained a short while in prayer before the Tabernacle did he turn toward his anxious community.

"Don't be frightened," he announced in calm,

clear tones. "In a few minutes we'll go together to safety."

Suddenly the young novice fell sobbing to his knees. "They'll kill my little brothers!" he cried frantically. "They'll make my mother a slave! Oh, Father! I've got to go to my family right away! I can't stay here!"

Hyacinth looked with compassion on the terrified novice, a Russian boy who had lived in mortal dread of the Tartars since childhood. Then he stepped forward and gently raised him to his feet.

"God will look after your family," he said, "but only if you have faith, if you remain here with the rest of us. Do you understand, little brother?"

At the sound of his superior's kindly voice and under the steady pressure of his hand, the boy's sickening fear began to fade. Still trembling, still white and shaken, he managed to speak.

"Yes, Father," he whispered. "I...I understand."

While the novice recovered himself, Hyacinth removed his Mass vestments, save for the stole, and donned his black mantle. Then he took the golden ciborium containing the consecrated Hosts out of the Tabernacle and once again addressed his little family.

"All will be well," he said. "Just follow me."

In a moment an orderly procession had formed in the chapel. Hyacinth was at the head, followed by the novices and then the older members of the community. No one spoke, and so the occasional screams of the approaching Tartars were all the more audible. Then as the long double line of black-and-white-clad figures began to move toward the door, a new voice was heard.

"Hyacinth, my son! Will you abandon me to the Tartars?"

Every head turned. A woman had spoken! And in soft and lovely tones! But who was she? And where? Then suddenly the Tartars were all but forgotten, for the friars saw that Hyacinth was standing before the alabaster statue of Our Lady which Vladimir Rurikovitch had presented to the community several years ago. He was standing there with puzzled eyes.

"Mother, what else can I do?" he was saying. "Your statue is too heavy to carry far."

For a moment all was silence. Then once again the lovely voice echoed through the chapel. "Have no fear, Hyacinth. My Son will ease the burden. In His Name, take me with you!"

"HAVE NO FEAR, HYACINTH.
MY SON WILL EASE THE BURDEN."

CHAPTER 14

THE STORM

ALREADY HYACINTH was carrying the Blessed Sacrament in his right hand, but with faith all things are possible. Quickly he reached up with his left arm, embraced the fifty-five pound statue, lifted it as though it were a feather, and started for the door.

"Now we go in real safety," he said.

Thus the entire community passed from the monastery into the streets. No one spoke, and at first it seemed that Kiev was deserted. Long ago every man, woman and child had taken refuge in the fortifications high above the city. Then suddenly the ominous quiet was broken. Out of nowhere appeared a dozen Tartars, armed with swords and flaming torches. With one accord these charged boldly into the friars' ranks.

"Christians!" they screamed. "Burn them! Kill them!"

But the squat, yellow-skinned warriors had not counted on a power greater than their own. Instantaneously they were struck powerless and found themselves forced to kneel meekly before the two lines of religious. The swords clattered harmlessly to the ground, the torches sputtered and went out. Fear was stamped on every pagan face. Never had these slanting oriental eyes beheld such a sight: a group of Christian friars passing harmlessly through their midst with a strong one at their head—a strong one whose left arm carried a great statue while his right hand gripped a golden vessel that shone like the sun.

"It's the god of the Christians!" they muttered. "He's going to kill us!"

But Hyacinth had no intention of harming this advance group of the enemy, who apparently had swum the icy river with orders to destroy whatever they could in Kiev. Looking neither to right nor to left, he guided his friars through the deserted streets toward the Dnieper. Then, with a little smile, he faced his companions.

"Look, my sons! The Tartar armies are still encamped. And I think they are wondering why their brothers allow us to stand here unharmed."

All eyes looked across the water. Small fires were burning before the tents that stretched for miles along the opposite shore. And as a sign that the friars had been seen and that the Tartars could hardly wait to begin their wholesale massacre of Christians, hundreds of arrows arched into the sky. But they fell ineffectually into the water, since the distance was too great for bow-and-arrow warfare.

Suddenly a stern expression crossed Hyacinth's face. "The heathen have given their sign," he said.

"Now we shall give ours. Come, my sons. Down to the water!"

Without hesitation the friars followed Hyacinth to the river's edge. Already their eyes had witnessed two wonders this day—the lessening in weight of Our Lady's statue, so that it could be carried quite easily by one arm, and the miraculous escape from the small band of Tartars. Now apparently there was to be a third miracle. But what? And where?

In just a few minutes the two questions were answered. Hyacinth reached the river and pointed downstream. "Come," he said. "Let us show the enemy that we are really sons of the True God."

Somehow all present realized what was about to happen. Through Hyacinth's prayers, God would suspend the laws of nature and allow each of them to walk safely upon the water. They would not cross to the opposite bank, since the Tartars were encamped here, but they would journey in midstream away from Kiev—and this as a sign that Heaven was protecting them.

Thus it happened, and a great shout arose from the Tartar hordes as they observed the wonderful sight. But Hyacinth did not even turn his head. Because it was the Will of the Heavenly Father, he and his companions were now escaping from Kiev by miraculous means. But what suffering was in store for those being left behind! Only a handful—including the family of the young novice who had been so terrified that morning—would miss death or capture. Even Fathers Albert and Dominic, two of Hyacinth's sons, were soon to undergo torture and

death. Recently they had gone to preach in Cher-
nigof, little realizing that the Tartars would strike
during their absence and that when they tried to
return to Kiev they would be set upon and killed.

"Dearest Mother, grant that these children go
straight to Heaven!" Hyacinth prayed. "And help us
to go there, too—when our time comes!"

Eventually the little group of fugitives found
haven in Lemberg, the large city in eastern Galicia
which some years ago had offered Hyacinth land
and funds for a monastery. Here Our Lady's statue
resumed its normal weight and presently was
installed in a fitting shrine. For weeks Hyacinth was
kept busy preaching to the crowds that flocked to
the shrine, but finally he judged it well to continue
on to Poland. It was now January, 1241, and according to the messengers who came in and out of the
city, the Tartar invasion was in full swing. Mangu's
army had completely destroyed Kiev, and other
Tartar forces were swarming westward. In a week
or two Sandomierz would be under siege. Then
would come Cracow's hour of peril.

"I must go home," Hyacinth told his friends in
Lemberg. "Possibly I can be of some help there."

As he set out westward on the one-hundred-and-
eighty-mile journey to Cracow, accompanied by
Godinus and Florian, the heart of the famous
preacher was heavy. What dreadful times these
were! And how inhuman the Tartars!

"I've heard that they fight in groups of ten," said
Godinus one morning as he and Florian tried in
vain to comfort their beloved superior. "If one of

the ten is cowardly, the other nine are sentenced to death."

"Yes, and if ten should be found wanting, a hundred are condemned to die. Oh, no wonder the Tartars are so ruthless in warfare, Father! They are trained for it from childhood!"

Childhood! The word was like a bugle call to Hyacinth! If someone could have reached the Tartars generations ago there would not be this horrible warfare now. If someone could reach the children of the whole world, teaching them that lasting happiness is to be found only in loving God and doing His Will...

"What is it, Father?" asked Florian, struck by the sudden radiance in Hyacinth's eyes. "Do you see something?"

Hyacinth smiled. "Yes, but nothing really new, Brother. Only this time it is clearer than ever before."

And then Hyacinth began to speak about children—the hope of the future. When the dreadful Tartar invasion was over, they must be reached. They must be told about God and taught to love Him; otherwise new and more dreadful wars would be visited upon the world. Yes, preaching friars must go out to every corner of Europe—even to Asia, home of the dreaded Tartars. And they must go with the same message for rich and poor, for strong and weak: *God made man to know Him, to love Him and to serve Him in this life and to be happy with Him forever in the next.*

"That's all, Brother. If we teach the little ones

that there is just one way for them to be happy in this world—by giving themselves completely into God's hands to do whatever work He has in store for them—oh, what wonderful results there will be in the future!"

There was hope in Hyacinth's voice, and in the weeks that followed Florian and Godinus often called his cheering words to mind. There was need for this, since by the spring of 1241 the Tartar hordes had advanced as far west as Breslau. Sandomierz had been taken, and Cracow, and now thousands of fertile acres lay pillaged and burned.

"But it's nothing to what the people have suffered," Florian confided to Godinus one day. "Oh, Brother! Sometimes I wonder if the Tartars are really human!"

The barbarian hordes hardly seemed human. They were masters at torture, and it was nothing unusual for one of their captives to be dragged to a post, run through with a lance, then shot at with arrows—and all this solely for the amusement of the Tartar chieftains. If the prisoner survived, fresh tortures were in store for him. Wooden splinters would be driven under his fingernails and then set afire; or he would be skinned alive. Finally, there were the many times when the Tartars cried out for additional brutality. Then the prisoners were roasted to death over a slow fire and their limbs hacked off with blunt axes.

As Hyacinth made his way back into devastated Poland, he did his best to comfort the stricken people. In firm tones he predicted that the present sorrow would pass and that it would result in great spiritual good.

"But when, Father?" was the universal lament, for everyone was heartsick and fearful. "Don't you know that the Tartars have now reached Breslau?"

Hyacinth did know this, but just the same he continued to preach faith and confidence and abandonment to the Will of God. He admitted that Poland had suffered dreadfully in recent months but prophesied that she would not die from her wounds. Rather, she would rise up again soon, and because of her present brave stand against the barbarians, western Europe would be saved for Christianity. Never would Batu's heathen hordes impose their harsh rule in Germany, Italy, France or Spain.

In April, 1241, word came that the preaching friar was right. At Liegnitz, some forty miles west of Breslau, the Tartars had locked in battle with the armies of Duke Henry the Pious, son of the saintly Duchess Hedwig of Silesia. As usual, the heathen had triumphed, with the young Duke losing his life. But this time the defeat of the Christian armies did not result in a further westward plunge by the Tartars. For some unknown reason the barbarians seemed loath to take advantage of their victory and overnight began to withdraw from Liegnitz.

"They're going back to Asia!" was the joyful announcement that soon was sweeping the country. "The prayers of the Duchess Hedwig have been heard!"

"Yes, and her son was a true martyr," insisted others. "He gave his life to save us."

There was no other explanation for the Tartars' decision to withdraw from Silesia and Poland. However, there were few to feast their eyes on the sight of the departing barbarians, since the Tartars were famous for their ability to move their huge caravans at night and with scarcely a sound. In fact, one day they would be burning a captured city, torturing prisoners, rounding up women and children, seizing cattle and crops. The next day it was as though both conquerors and conquered had vanished from the face of the earth.

"The barbarians have thousands of the swiftest horses in the world," was one explanation. "That's why they can move with the speed of lightning."

"The barbarians are devils from Hell," was another version. "Lucifer himself has trained them to fly through the darkness."

Be that as it may, the Tartars' withdrawal from Liegnitz was hidden, swift, complete. It was almost unbelievable, and for months there was a lurking suspicion throughout both Poland and Silesia that they would return. Then, finally, Hyacinth's word prevailed.

"God has given us several years of peace," he said confidently. "My brothers, let us use this time to rebuild our ruined cities."

Several years of peace! Grim-faced men and women repeated the phrase slowly, fearfully, realizing only too well that it carried within itself the germ of fresh sorrow. For what was truly permanent about "several years" of peace?

"Oh, Father! You mean that our suffering isn't

finished yet? that the Tartars will return?"

Hyacinth nodded. "Yes; in 1259, two years after my death. But take courage. They will never attack in such strength as at Liegnitz."

So the huge task of rebuilding got underway. Peasants went back to their burned acres, and slowly hope returned to the North. By the end of 1241 Hyacinth was one of the busiest men in Poland, for there was scarcely a church or monastery of his Order which had escaped destruction. Cracow, Sandomierz, Troppau—everywhere the story was the same.

"Bishop Stanislaus must have welcomed hundreds of fellow martyrs to Heaven since the barbarians came," the friar told himself. "Every day we discover new bodies in the ruins."

Yes, the Tartars had always despised Christianity and therefore had taken special pains to violate every place of worship they could find. Of course much of the evidence had been destroyed when the churches and monasteries were burned, but generally one or two signs of heathen malice remained— a twisted crucifix, for instance, the corpus smashed into a hundred pieces, or statues toppled from their pedestals and covered with filth, or even the bodies of priests and lay Brothers, strangled, mutilated, burned.

"Oh, Blessed Mother, we have to begin our work all over again now!" Hyacinth thought. "Please give us the strength to carry on bravely, no matter what the hardships!"

Hardships! There were many of these, and from

the start Cracow's famous preacher knew that of himself he could never hope to bear even the smallest. Rather, he must act like a little child and place himself and his work in the hands of the Heavenly Father. What if he was fifty-six years of age? The way he had chosen would always be the surest way for anyone to obtain success and lasting peace of mind.

The following summer there was a good chance for Hyacinth to test the depth of his peace of mind, for a messenger from Breslau brought word that Ceslaus was dead. He had gone to his reward on July 16, aged fifty-eight years.

"Those dreadful days last spring when the Tartars were destroying Breslau were too much for our good Father," said the messenger. "He never recovered his strength."

Hyacinth nodded. " Tell me all about my brother," he said quietly, "particularly what happened to him since the Provincial Chapter at Sandomierz four years ago. That was the last time we met."

The messenger obeyed, although with difficulty. Father Ceslaus had done so much in the last four years! He had preached, taught, heard Confessions, guided dozens of souls in the spiritual life. He had looked after the poor, too—seeing that Breslau's needy were supplied with the necessities of life. Many times there had even been talk of miracles. . .

"They say his prayers revived a boy whose body had lain eight days at the bottom of the Oder river," said the messenger slowly. "And of course there are many other wonderful stories, too."

Hyacinth listened like one in a dream. Ceslaus was dead! Rather, Ceslaus was a saint in Heaven! How wonderful!

"Go on," he whispered. "Tell me more."

So the messenger described Ceslaus' heroism during the dark days when Breslau had been under siege by the Tartars. In the midst of the battle he had mounted to the city walls and stood there in full view of the enemy, arms outstretched in prayer, heedless of the poisoned arrows flying thick and fast about him.

"He offered himself as a victim for the sins of the Tartars," explained the messenger. "And as he prayed, we all saw that a strange light was shining about him. The Tartars saw it, too, and many threw down their weapons and would fight no more. A few days later they moved on to Liegnitz. Of course they destroyed most of Breslau, but thousands of us were saved because Father Ceslaus had arranged that we should take refuge in the higher part of the city. It was surely because of his prayers that the Tartars never made a real effort to reach us."

There was no doubt about it: Ceslaus had been regarded as a saint even in his lifetime. Now that he was dead, all Breslau was sure of it. Hyacinth was sure of it, too, and long after the messenger had taken his departure he knelt in his cell and begged God to allow Ceslaus to help him in his work.

"My brother is no longer an imperfect man, dear Lord, for his soul has reached the measure of perfection which You designed for it from all eternity.

"IN THE MIDST OF THE BATTLE
HE HAD MOUNTED TO THE CITY WALLS..."

Oh, please let his perfect prayers win new graces for Poland! You see, he loved his country so much, and these days the people are in great need of heavenly helpers. . ."

As the weeks passed, Hyacinth felt convinced that God had granted his request. Surely Ceslaus was now one of Poland's special patrons. In company with Bishop Stanislaus, he would do all that he could to promote the welfare of his beloved land. Yet while Hyacinth rejoiced at this, his soul was heavy on another score. Ceslaus Odrowatz might be enshrined in Polish hearts as a holy servant of God, since his earthly work was over and Divine Providence allowed miracles to take place at his tomb in Breslau. But was this any reason why Hyacinth Odrowatz should also be considered a saint and wonderworker? that men and women should flock to him as he supervised the rebuilding of Cracow's Monastery of the Holy Trinity and beg that he cure them of this and that ailment?

"Dear friends, why not spend five minutes in honest prayer before the Blessed Sacrament?" he urged. "That would be of far more help than any poor words of mine."

The citizens of Cracow listened respectfully but continued their pleas. The result? Hyacinth's kindly heart was touched, and he agreed to place his hand upon the sick, to pray for this and that favor. Soon the faith of his friends was rewarded, and day after day the streets echoed to joyful shouts as cripples walked, the blind saw, the deaf heard, the dumb spoke.

"Father Hyacinth is the greatest man in all Poland," was the universal cry. "God has given him the grace to do *anything* for those who ask his help!"

On September 27, 1243, a pale-faced young mother came to the Monastery of the Holy Trinity in Cracow. Her name was Vitoslava, and in her arms she carried twin baby boys.

"Please let me see Father Hyacinth," she begged the lay Brother who opened the door. "I . . . I want to ask him a favor."

The Brother smiled. "Have you forgotten about the celebration at the Cathedral in honor of Bishop Stanislaus? Father Hyacinth has gone there this morning to preach the chief sermon."

Vitoslava did not seem to understand. "Look," she whispered, removing a light veil from the children's faces. "Look at my babies!"

The lay Brother leaned forward, then drew back with an exclamation of dismay. "Why, they're blind!" he muttered. "Poor little things!"

"*Blind?* You mean they were born without eyes!" choked the mother, replacing the veil with trembling fingers. "Oh, I can hardly bear it!"

A sharp pang shot through the lay Brother. What tragedy was here! What anguish! But he hid his true feelings as best he could and pointed toward the Cathedral.

"Father Hyacinth has worked hundreds of miracles," he said comfortingly. "If you go to him now, he will surely help you, too. Only make sure of one thing."

Great tears were rolling down Vitoslava's face as she cradled her infant sons in her arms. "What?" she whispered brokenly.

The lay Brother's voice took on solemn tones. "Ask for your favor in the name of Bishop Stanislaus, that he may be canonized soon. Then Father Hyacinth will pray with such strength and love that God will grant whatever he asks—no matter how impossible!"

CHAPTER 15

APOSTLE OF THE NORTH

THE LAY Brother was right. That same day all Cracow resounded to the wonderful news that Hyacinth's prayers had worked another miracle. Vitoslava's twin boys, born without eyes, were now like other children. On an instant they had been made whole by the good preacher's blessing.

"It's almost too much to believe!" the young woman told her husband, laughing and crying as she caressed first one child and then another. "Oh, how can we repay Father Hyacinth for all his kindness?"

Her husband, still shaken by the recent miracle, shook his head. "We can never repay him," he said slowly. "But maybe it would help if we did what he told us."

"You mean consecrate the boys to Our Lady?"

"That's right. Don't you remember that Father Hyacinth said all Christian parents should do this for each of their children?"

Vitoslava nodded. "I remember. He believes that

"IT'S ALMOST TOO MUCH TO BELIEVE!"

Our Lady gives very special graces to the little ones entrusted to her care."

So it was that the next day the young couple's twin boys were consecrated to the Blessed Virgin, together with several other children whose parents had heard of the astounding miracle. Hyacinth was delighted, since his love for Our Lady was even greater now than it had been in his youthful days. He liked nothing better than to praise her in his sermons. Indeed, his followers had become known throughout Poland not only as the Friars Preachers but also as the Brothers of Mary.

"Whatever good I have been able to do has always come through Our Lady," he often insisted. "She has never abandoned me."

The havoc wrought by the Tartars was slowly mended. Once again churches and monasteries lifted their crosses to the sky, and black-and-white-clad friars preached God's Truth in Poland, Pomerania and Prussia. Indeed, in their General Chapter of 1245 the Cistercian monks officially renounced all missionary work in northern Europe. Henceforth they would retire to the seclusion of their monasteries, and the apostolic work of preaching and teaching which they had carried on for so many years would belong exclusively to the sons of Dominic and Francis.

This did not mean that the Cistercians withdrew entirely from the field, however. The General Chapter of 1245 provided that each priest and lay Brother should remember in special prayer those friars who tramped the length and breadth of northern Europe in God's service. Each day the priests were to recite seven psalms, the lay Brothers seven Our Fathers, and both with the same intention: that Christianity should flourish in the wake of the preaching friars.

Hyacinth was deeply grateful for the prayers of the Cistercians and for those of his other friends, for well he knew that they would win for him many graces. But as he gave thanks for the decision of the Cistercians at their General Chapter, a messenger arrived from Breslau and another from Oppeln. Fathers Henry and Herman, those two companions of his youth, were dead!

"Father Henry died like a saint," announced the messenger from Breslau in awed tones. "All through his agony he kept his eyes on the crucifix. Then at the last he turned to those who were kneeling about his bed and whispered these words: 'The Devil tries to tempt my faith, but I believe in God the Father, the Son and Holy Ghost.' Then he died—oh, so peacefully!"

"Father Herman died like a saint, too," put in the messenger from Oppeln. "In fact, on the day of his passing a radiant cross appeared in the sky and shone so brightly as to dim the sun. Everyone saw it and marveled. But there was great sorrow, too. You see, no one in Oppeln wanted to lose Father Herman. He was everybody's friend—so kind, so wise!"

Hyacinth could smile at this, recalling those days in Rome when a youthful Herman had scarcely known how to write his own name, let alone how to preach and instruct others. But the ways of God were wonderful indeed. Because Herman had been truly humble, he had been allowed to do great things for souls. Divine Providence had even arranged that he be placed in charge of Hyacinth's first monastery, the one founded in Friesach. Later, the young German had received so many graces, such floods of heavenly Wisdom, that he had been able to preach in several languages and thus bring many to God.

"Herman, my son, may your good soul rest in peace!" Hyacinth whispered. "Henry, my son, pray for me—that I may be made worthy of the promises of Christ!"

As the months passed, the Monastery of the Holy Trinity was completely rebuilt, and one morning Hyacinth thrilled to the fact that at last he might undertake his missionary labors once again. He was sixty years old, the age when most men seek to retire from active life, but thoughts of a well-earned rest never entered his head. There was so much to be done for souls! Vilna, for instance—the largest city in Lithuania—what better spot was there than this in which to establish a monastery of preaching friars?

"I'll go to Vilna," he told himself firmly. "God willing, many people in Lithuania will be glad to hear about the Christian Faith."

So on foot, and accompanied by the faithful Brother Florian, Hyacinth set out on the four-hundred-mile journey from Cracow to Vilna. He was in good spirits as he said farewell to his brethren at Holy Trinity, but it was with heavy hearts that these saw their beloved superior depart. When he had finally disappeared in the distance, they looked at one another solemnly.

"We should have tried to stop him," said Father Peter, the procurator. "These long journeys are meant only for younger men."

The Prior agreed. "Of course. But what young priests have we whom God has blessed with the gift of miracles? None! And you know what a great part miracles play in winning pagans to Christianity."

The Prior spoke the truth. In Paris, Bologna and other centers of learning, the Friars Preachers were converting hundreds from heresy by dint of powerful logic. Their sermons in church and public square, their lectures in the Universities, were winning the best minds in Europe to the cause of Christ. But in the far North God had given Hyacinth other means to do a similar work. He had endowed him with powers bestowed upon only a few men, so that he walked quite freely upon the rivers, raised the dead to life, was familiar with all tongues and dialects, and performed other startling feats. And why? For one reason only: that the pagan tribes, as yet unable to read or to follow any but the simplest course of instruction, might understand that the Catholic Faith was the one true religion and be led to embrace it.

Months passed, and finally word reached Cracow that Hyacinth had been successful in establishing a monastery in Vilna. Now he was planning to go to Russia once more, believing that preaching friars would find a fertile field for their labors in Smolensk, Moscow and Vladimir.

"Father Hyacinth is a true apostle," said the Prior of Holy Trinity reverently. "He never rests."

The good religious did not realize how truly he spoke, for as the years rolled by Hyacinth seemed to take on fresh energy. Not content with evangelizing Lithuania and northern Russia, he turned his steps once more toward Kiev. But not to stay. No, only to rebuild the monastery destroyed by the Tartars, gather together a few friars, fill them with his own hunger for souls, then send them eastwards into the vast stretches of Asia.

"He wants to found monasteries in Persia, Turkestan and Tibet," went one rumor. "Even in China."

"Yes, and the Holy Father is going to make him a Bishop," went another.

But Hyacinth steadfastly refused all such honors, even though three of his sons had been raised to the episcopacy in 1236. He insisted that his work still was to found as many monasteries of preaching friars as possible, place a younger man in charge, then move on to fresh fields. He would follow this pattern as long as God gave him the necessary strength.

By the year 1256 Cracow's famous preacher was affectionately known by thousands of people as "The Apostle of the North." His miracles were on every tongue, exceeding by far those of Bishop Stanislaus, whose canonization finally had taken place in 1253. As for his travels—who could keep track of them? One time he would be reported to be preaching in Russia, the next in Sweden, so that there was scarcely a person in the entire Northland who did not cherish the hope of some day meeting him. After all, what a privilege to see and hear a man who had raised the dead to life, who possessed the gift of tongues, who had been a friend and disciple of Father Dominic de Guzman!

At Easter of 1257 a thrill of real joy ran through Cracow when it was announced that Father Hyacinth finally had returned to the Monastery of the Holy Trinity. Not wishing to attract attention, he had entered the city in the dead of night. But very quickly the joy was tempered by fear. It was the spring of 1257, which meant that in a few months Father Hyacinth would be seventy-two years old.

"He always said he would die at this age," one person told another. "Oh, what a dreadful thing his passing will be!"

Hearing the rumors and noting the many anxious glances cast upon him whenever he ventured into the streets, Hyacinth smiled. Yet one July morning he surprised everyone by announcing that he hoped to be able to spend a few days in the country. Some old friends had invited him to celebrate the feast of Saint James the Greater at their estate in Sernik.

"They've already sent a servant and their young son Vislaus to be my escorts," he told the Prior. "With your permission, Father, we'll leave early tomorrow morning."

The Prior's eyes widened. What was this? Cracow's

famous preacher was asking for a permission like
the youngest novice? But even as he started to
smile, his face grew grave. "Of course you may leave
tomorrow, Father Hyacinth. Or whenever you wish.
Yet are you sure you're really strong enough to
make the trip? Sernik is several miles distant, you
know, and across the Raba river. . ."

Hyacinth nodded. "I'm more than strong enough
to go to Sernik, Father Prior, and back again, too.
Never fear about that."

So, early the next morning, after offering the
Holy Sacrifice, Hyacinth came to the front door of
the monastery, where sixteen-year-old Vislaus and
an elderly man-servant were waiting for him. But
as he noted that three horses stood a short distance
off, richly saddled and bridled, he smiled and shook
his head.

"I'm just a poor friar, my son, accustomed to
traveling on foot. However, wouldn't it be possible. . .that is, for a little way at least. . .that you
share my poverty? You see, I want to hear all about
you and your family."

Vislaus swallowed his amazement that this white-
haired priest, home to die after hundreds of missionary journeys, was still so faithful to his vow of
poverty. But greatly as he would have liked to urge
Hyacinth to go to Sernik in comfort, something in
the friar's bearing forbade it.

"Whatever you wish, Father," he said quickly.
Then, to the servant: "John, will you go ahead with
the horses, please? But stop from time to time so
that we can catch up with you. That way you'll be

able to have a little visit with Father Hyacinth, too."

In the course of the journey, sixteen-year-old Vislaus fell completely captive to Hyacinth's friendli-
ness and rejoiced that his family had sent him to
act as guide. Never before had he found it so easy
to open his heart to anyone. Why, somehow it was
as though the good priest could read his innermost
thoughts! Then suddenly the boy turned toward his
new-found friend.

"My mother says you've raised several dead people to life, Father. Is that really true?"

The friar hesitated. Then he nodded gravely.
"Yes, my son. For His own good reasons, God has
given me that grace many times."

Vislaus clasped his hands. "Oh, Father! Do you
suppose you could do it again while you're staying
with us in Sernik?"

Hyacinth's exclamation of dismay was checked by
the youthful innocence shining in the boy's eyes.
But when the friar spoke, his voice was very serious.
"You don't understand, Vislaus. Of himself, no man
has real power over life or death, or over any of
the other laws of nature. Only when God's glory
may be furthered is there a question of asking for,
and receiving, such a dangerous gift."

The boy was quick to take his cue from Hyacinth,
so that now his voice also was serious. "Father, I
think I'd be a much better person if I could see
a real miracle," he protested respectfully. "That's all
I meant when I asked if you could work another."

"You mean your faith would be stronger?"

"Oh, yes, Father! Particularly if it was a matter

of a dead person's being raised to life!"

Once again Hyacinth was silent for a moment. "All that is necessary for our salvation is to love God and to do His Will," he murmured finally. Then, with a friendly pat on his young friend's shoulder, he announced that the boy had walked far enough. Now he ought to rejoin John and continue the journey on horseback.

"Tell your mother that I'll arrive before sundown, Vislaus, and that I'm very grateful for her invitation."

The boy hesitated. "Yes, Father. But may I also tell her that God is going to let you work some kind of a wonder in Sernik?"

Hyacinth shook a warning finger. What a persistent lad was Vislaus! "Tell your mother what I just told you," he said firmly, "that the only reason for miracles is to promote God's glory."

So young Vislaus hurried forward to rejoin John, and soon the two had disappeared on their horses in a cloud of dust. Then, as was his custom while walking alone, Hyacinth recollected himself and began to recite the Psalms. Sometimes he spoke the words aloud, at others was silent, scarcely noticing the passage of the hours or of the miles. But towards sunset he lifted his eyes and saw that he was approaching the Raba river. Sernik was now only a short distance away.

Even as he rejoiced, a group of horsemen suddenly appeared around a bend in the road. They were riding very fast, and at once a cold fear clutched the friar's heart. Something terrible had happened! And to Vislaus!

His fear was confirmed. A few hours earlier John and his young master had reached the river. The boy had been very eager to tell his family that Father Hyacinth was on his way to spend the feast of Saint James with them. So, to save time, he had decided to use an old bridge at the stream's narrowest point.

"I tried to stop him, Father," moaned John, half beside himself with grief, "but it was no use. He wanted to get home quickly, and so he insisted on riding across the bridge, even though it was half-rotten."

"Yes? And what happened then?"

The old man hid his face in his hands. "The bridge gave way, Father, and my young master fell from his horse and was swept under by the current. Oh, Mother of God! The boy had his whole life before him, while I . . . an old worthless wretch . . ."

John's grief was as nothing to that of Vislaus' mother, however. This poor woman, whose name was Primislava, all but collapsed when she caught sight of the famous preacher whom she had known since childhood and whose visit she had been anticipating with such great pleasure.

"Oh, Father, what am I going to do?" she choked. "I don't even know where my boy's body is!"

Hyacinth did his best to comfort Primislava, but to no avail. She was shattered by grief. Vislaus was her only child. Finally Hyacinth spoke again. "We'll pray," he said gently. "We'll ask the Heavenly Father, in the Name of His own Son, Jesus Christ, to give your boy back to you."

Silence descended upon the little group as Hyacinth bowed his head and remained in prayer for several minutes. Then suddenly there was a shout. A dark object, half submerged, was rapidly floating in to shore. It might very well be. . .

"It *is* the young master's body!" cried John.

CHAPTER 16

THE MESSAGE

PRIMISLAVA TURNED eagerly to Hyacinth, filled with new hope. "Give Vislaus back to me *alive!*" she begged. "Please, Father!"

"Yes," whispered John, his old hands trembling as he gazed at the boy he had loved, now stretched out on the ground before him, cold in death. "It would. . .it would mean so much to all of us!"

Suddenly the voices of Primislava's friends and servants became to Hyacinth as the roar of a great wind. With tears and sobs each man and woman present was beseeching him to wrest from the Divine Mercy the great favor.

"If God grants what we ask, no one here will ever fall into grievous sin again!" cried John earnestly. "I swear it, Father!"

"Show us the power of the Blessed Virgin!" a young girl begged, her arms about Primislava, who was gazing at Hyacinth imploringly.

"Yes, Father," urged an old woman tearfully. "You've always said that Our Lady gives you everything you ask of her. . ."

Hyacinth's kindly heart could resist no longer. With faltering steps (he was weary from his long walk to Sernik) he advanced toward the lifeless body. Then he raised his hand in blessing.

"Vislaus, my son, give glory to God!" he commanded. "Return to life, in the Name of the Father, and of the Son, and of the Holy Ghost!"

For a moment there was silence. Then suddenly the crowd gasped. Slowly, very slowly, the body upon the ground was beginning to stir! As Primislava flung herself upon her knees beside her son, a great cry split the air.

"A miracle! Father Hyacinth has worked another miracle!"

"Yes!" shouted others joyfully. "Vislaus is alive after all!"

In the days that followed Cracow's famous preacher was besieged by throngs of the faithful, urging him to help them in this or that difficulty. Hyacinth did all he could, but when he finally returned home to the Monastery of the Holy Trinity, his strength was all but gone.

"Father, you must go to bed at once!" cried the Prior, alarmed at the change that a few days' absence had wrought. "You worked far too hard at Sernik."

Hyacinth smiled. "I'm quite all right, Father Prior. Just a little tired."

But on the feast of Saint Dominic all realized that Hyacinth's days were numbered. Apart from the fact that he was worn out with thirty-seven years of missionary labors, he no longer cared to live.

Indeed, his one great desire was to die as quickly as possible.

"And why? Because our good Father has had a glimpse of Heaven!" the Prior told the community in awed tones. "He's seen a little of the reward awaiting those who do God's Will, and now even the finest things in life are no more than dust and ashes."

"Tell us about the wonderful vision, Father," urged the Novice Master. "It will do us all good."

So the Prior began. He explained how one day recently Father Hyacinth, as he was concluding the Holy Sacrifice, had found himself in the center of a bright ray of light. It had streamed down upon him from some mysterious source above the altar, and as he looked up, he had been amazed to find that hundreds of angels and saints were also enfolded in the strange glow. Suddenly there was an even greater radiance, and Heaven itself opened before him. Then the saints and angels divided and ranged themselves in two lines, facing one another. At the end of the glittering passageway was a golden throne.

"Our Lady was seated on the throne," said the Prior reverently, "and Our Lord stood beside her. The air was filled with the most beautiful music as the saints and angels joined in praise of Mother and Son. Then suddenly the perfect harmony died away. All was silence, and Our Lord placed a splendid crown upon His Mother's head. It seemed to be made of flowers and stars."

The community listened in breathless astonishment as the Prior described the scene which followed. With a smile the Blessed Virgin had taken the glittering crown from her own head and presented it to Hyacinth.

"This is for you," she had said, "the symbol of eternal life." And as she finished speaking, the saints and angels resumed their heavenly song, their faces shining with such light and happiness that Hyacinth could hardly bear to look upon them. Indeed, only one thought filled his mind. He wanted to finish his earthly work at once, so that he might be numbered among these blessed ones for all eternity.

As the days passed the priests and lay Brothers of Holy Trinity went about their duties in deep thought. Father Hyacinth's vision of Heaven, as related by the Prior, had made an enormous impression upon them, and now even the smallest task was seen in a new light. Its faithful accomplishment was nothing more than a coin wherewith to purchase everlasting joys.

"Of course, we've always known that this was so," said one young priest slowly. "The trouble is, we've never thought about it enough. But now—well, I'm happy to say that I can't get the idea out of my mind."

"Yes," put in another. "And that crown of flowers and stars is far more than it seems. It's only a sign, and a very small sign, too, of all the joys possessed by the blessed in Heaven."

His companion nodded. "I know. Why, if we spent our whole lives in listing the good things God has provided for those who serve Him faithfully in this world, we'd have only a few poor samples."

As the warm August days succeeded one another, Hyacinth grew very weak. But he still insisted on offering the Holy Sacrifice each morning and on attending the recitation of the Divine Office in choir. However, a few minutes before midnight on the eve of the Assumption, he called for Brother Florian, who was watching beside his bed. It seemed that his strength was about gone but that nevertheless he wanted to join his brethren in chanting Matins and Lauds of the great feast.

"I'll not be able to offer Mass tomorrow in Our Lady's honor," he whispered, "but surely I can sing her praises with the others?"

Brother Florian tried to persuade his beloved superior to rest, but to no avail. Hyacinth insisted on being led to his usual place in the chapel, where for the last time he joined in the chanting of the beautiful psalms and other prayers of the Feast of the Assumption. And as the night air filled with the holy and familiar sound, he was transported back across the years. It was no longer August 15, 1257, and he a white-haired old man with the strength gone out of his limbs. No, it was August 15, 1224. He was thirty-nine years old and Prior of the newly dedicated Monastery of the Holy Trinity—with his heart and mind full of wonderful plans for evangelizing the whole of northern Europe. Then suddenly a sweet voice rang out:

"Rejoice, Hyacinth! Your prayers are pleasing to my Son! From now on all that you ask of Him in

my name will be granted!"

Hyacinth smiled at the remembrance of the wonderful night when Our Lady had spoken to him. Oh, how truly she had kept her promise! Never since then had he asked anything in her name and been refused. The miracles, the conversions, the success of his friars as missionaries—all had been due to her kindness.

"Thank you, dear Lady," he whispered. "Thank you so much!"

Presently the chanting ceased, and Brother Florian made ready to lead Hyacinth back to his cell. But the latter held out a restraining hand. He would not be strong enough to offer the Holy Sacrifice on this great feast, but at least he could receive Our Lord in the Holy Eucharist.

"Perhaps Father Prior would be willing to offer his own Mass now and to give me Holy Communion," he said softly. "Will you ask him, my son?"

Naturally the Prior was willing, and so instead of returning to their cells to resume their interrupted sleep, the religious of Holy Trinity remained in the chapel. They would assist at this Mass and take their rest later.

At first all was quiet in the candle-lit sanctuary, save when the Prior raised his voice in the prayers of the Mass and the assembled community responded. Then one after another the friars found themselves choking back their tears. Their glances had strayed to Hyacinth kneeling near the altar steps, and the sight was too much to bear in silence. Why, the old man's face was actually glowing as he

". . . NEVER NOTICING THAT HIS FALTERING HANDS
WERE MAKING THE SAME MOTIONS
AS THOSE OF THE PRIEST AT THE ALTAR."

assisted at this, his last Mass! He was completely lost to his surroundings, never even noticing that his faltering hands were making the same movements as those of the priest at the altar!

As the Offertory began, with the Prior raising to Heaven the paten bearing the host that soon would be turned into the Body of Christ, the Novice Master leaned quickly toward his neighbor. "Look at him now!" he whispered.

Every head turned, and then a reverent gasp broke out on all sides. Father Hyacinth had raised his hands, too! For still another time, and with all the love at his command, he was giving himself to the Eternal Father to do with as He pleased. Old, broken, dying, he was practicing what had always been his favorite devotion—complete abandonment to the Divine Will.

The Novice Master's neighbor wiped his eyes. "This is our Father's finest sermon," he murmured. "We must never forget it."

Presently Hyacinth received Holy Communion, and after a brief thanksgiving, he permitted Brother Florian to lead him back to his cell. As they moved slowly down the darkened corridors, the old man pressed his companion's hand.

"Our Lord has promised that I am to leave you," he said softly. "Oh, my son! Pray that it be soon!"

At these words Florian could barely control his grief. Of course Father Hyacinth was beloved by every priest and Brother in the monastery. For that matter, there would be universal mourning throughout the city when he died. But of all the men and women who loved him, surely none would suffer more at his passing than Florian himself.

"I've been with him since I was a boy!" he thought. "I've...I've hardly ever been away from him since he gave me the habit!"

It was true. During the past thirty-five years Florian had walked countless miles as Hyacinth's companion on the missions throughout the Northland. On these trips he had performed all the little domestic services that would make life easier for his beloved superior. In the great quest for souls he had followed bravely into the swamps of Masovia, into the dense forests of Pomerania and Prussia—heedless of the danger from starving wolfpacks. He had crossed rivers, mountains and the windswept plains of Poland and Russia. He had witnessed the many and miraculous results of Hyacinth's sermons and prayers. He had seen churches and monasteries built, then desecrated and burned by the ruthless Tartars. And now all this was in the past. He was home in Cracow, at the Monastery of the Holy Trinity, and his beloved superior was about to die.

"Oh, Father! What shall I do without you?" he murmured brokenly. "What will our country do?"

Hyacinth understood the great grief in his disciple's heart and once more pressed his hand. "Have patience, my son," he whispered. "I'll give you a message in a little while."

By noon all in the monastery realized that Hyacinth's life was fast ebbing away. He had received Extreme Unction and now lay quietly upon his bed, his fingers holding the plain wooden crucifix which the Prior had placed in them. Only a few religious were in the little cell, but the corridor outside was lined with kneeling figures. From his vantage point by Hyacinth's bed Brother Florian could see a few of these—their heads bowed, their lips moving in prayer. However, his eyes very rarely left Hyacinth's face. After all, hadn't his beloved friend promised to give him a message?

"Father, please don't forget!" he murmured from time to time. "I...we...*need* this message!"

Although Florian repeated these words frequently, it was not until around three o'clock that Hyacinth gave evidence that he had heard. Then, opening his eyes, he looked long and lovingly at his faithful companion.

"I have not forgotten," he said, and his voice was vibrant and sure—not at all like that of a dying man.

As Brother Florian listened, an unearthly radiance began to shine from Hyacinth's face. "I am going to Heaven now, my son, yet I shall be with you in spirit. Whenever you are in trouble, you are to call upon me and I will come to your aid. Do you understand?"

Florian choked back a sob. "Yes, Father. I . . . I understand."

Hyacinth sighed. "No, you do *not* understand. Why, you can barely speak for sorrow, because deep in your heart you believe that the blessed are far away from you! But it is not so, my son. Oh, no!"

Then Hyacinth gave his message. Yes, he was

about to die. But this only meant that from now on he could be of greater use to his friends. In Heaven he would be a perfect soul, utterly pleasing to God, and so his prayers would have even more power than upon earth.

"Have faith in what I tell you," he urged. "And try to believe that I shall never really leave Poland. I shall be with my beloved country until the end."

The Prior leaned forward anxiously. "Is our country to have many troubles in the future, Father?"

The dying friar nodded. "Yes. But all will turn out well, Father Prior. Have no fear of that."

Suddenly a change came over Hyacinth. The radiance did not fade from his eyes, but his voice became much weaker. With a farewell smile for his brethren he turned to the crucifix. Then he began to pray, in the opening verses of the Thirtieth Psalm:

"In Thee, O Lord, have I hoped, let me never be confounded; deliver me in Thy justice."

The community took up the familiar lines, so that soon a mighty surge of sound was filling the little room and the corridor outside.

"Bow down Thine ear to me: make haste to deliver me. Be Thou unto me a God, a protector, and a house of refuge, to save me.

"For Thou art my strength and my refuge; and for Thy Name's sake Thou wilt lead me, and nourish me.

"Thou wilt bring me out of this snare, which they have hidden for me: for Thou art my protector.

"Into Thy hands I commend my spirit: Thou hast redeemed me, O Lord, the God of Truth . . ."

Suddenly the Prior bent over the bed, then turned to the community. "Our good Father has gone," he said simply.

Florian looked up at his superior. "Not really," he whispered.

New York City
Feast of Saint Justin
April 14, 1945

ORDER FORM

Please send me:

Qty.	Stock No.	Title	Amount
_____	_____	_____	_____
_____	_____	_____	_____
_____	_____	_____	_____
_____	_____	_____	_____
_____	_____	_____	_____
_____	_____	_____	_____

U.S. & CAN. POST/HDLG:
If total order=$1-$10, add $3.00;
$10.01-$25, add $5.00; $25.01-$50, add $6.00;
$50.01-$75, add $7.00; $75.01-$150, add $8.00;
$150.01-up, add $10.00.

Subtotal _____

7% Sales Tax _____
(IL residents only)

Post./Hdlg. _____

TOTAL _____

Enclosed is my payment of _____ .

Please charge my:
☐ VISA   ☐ MasterCard   ☐ Discover

Account number _____

Expiration date: Month _____ Year _____

Signature _____
(Please do not send your card.)

Name_____

Street _____

City _____

State _____ Zip _____

TAN BOOKS AND PUBLISHERS, INC.
P.O. Box 424
Rockford, Illinois 61105
1-800-437-5876   **www.tanbooks.com**

By the same author . . .

6 GREAT CATHOLIC
BOOKS FOR CHILDREN

. . . and for all young people ages 10 to 100!!

1137 THE CHILDREN OF FATIMA—And Our Lady's Message to the World. 162 pp. PB. 15 Illus. Impr. The wonderful story of Our Lady's appearances to little Jacinta, Francisco and Lucia at Fatima in 1917.   11.00

1138 THE CURÉ OF ARS—The Story of St. John Vianney, Patron Saint of Parish Priests. 211 pp. PB. 38 Illus. Impr. The many adventures that met young St. John Vianney when he set out to become a priest.   13.00

1139 THE LITTLE FLOWER—The Story of St. Therese of the Child Jesus. 167 pp. PB. 24 Illus. Impr. Tells what happened when little Therese decided to become a saint.   11.00

1140 PATRON SAINT OF FIRST COMMUNICANTS—The Story of Blessed Imelda Lambertini. 85 pp. PB. 14 Illus. Impr. Tells of the wonderful miracle God worked to answer little Imelda's prayer.   8.00

1141 THE MIRACULOUS MEDAL—The Story of Our Lady's Appearances to St. Catherine Labouré. 107 pp. PB. 21 Illus. Impr. The beautiful story of what happened when young Sister Catherine saw Our Lady.   9.00

1142 ST. LOUIS DE MONTFORT—The Story of Our Lady's Slave. 211 pp. PB. 20 Illus. Impr. The remarkable story of the priest who went around helping people become "slaves" of Jesus through Mary.   13.00

1136 ALL 6 BOOKS ABOVE (Reg. 65.00)   THE SET: 52.00

Prices subject to change.

U.S. & CAN. POST./HDLG.: $1-$10, add $3;
$10.01-$25, add $5; $25.01-$50, add $6; $50.01-$75, add $7;
$75.01-$150, add $8; $150.01 or more, add $10.

At your Bookdealer or direct from the Publisher.
Toll Free 1-800-437-5876   **Fax 815-226-7770**

6 <u>MORE</u> GREAT CATHOLIC BOOKS FOR CHILDREN

. . . and for all young people ages 10 to 100!!

1200 **SAINT THOMAS AQUINAS**—The Story of "The Dumb Ox." 81 pp. PB. 16 Illus. Impr. The remarkable story of how St. Thomas, called in school "The Dumb Ox," became the greatest Catholic teacher ever.   8.00

1201 **SAINT CATHERINE OF SIENA**—The Story of the Girl Who Saw Saints in the Sky. 65 pp. PB. 13 Illus. The amazing life of the most famous Catherine in the history of the Church.   7.00

1202 **SAINT HYACINTH OF POLAND**—The Story of The Apostle of the North. 189 pp. PB. 16 Illus. Impr. Shows how the holy Catholic Faith came to Poland, Lithuania, Prussia, Scandinavia and Russia.   13.00

1203 **SAINT MARTIN DE PORRES**—The Story of The Little Doctor of Lima, Peru. 122 pp. PB. 16 Illus. Impr. The incredible life and miracles of this black boy who became a great saint.   10.00

1204 **SAINT ROSE OF LIMA**—The Story of The First Canonized Saint of the Americas. 132 pp. PB. 13 Illus. Impr. The remarkable life of the little Rose of South America.   10.00

1205 **PAULINE JARICOT**—Foundress of the Living Rosary and The Society for the Propagation of the Faith. 244 pp. PB. 21 Illus. Impr. The story of a rich young girl and her many spiritual adventures.   15.00

1206 ALL 6 BOOKS ABOVE (Reg. 63.00)   THE SET: 50.00

Prices subject to change.

U.S. & CAN. POST./HDLG.: $1-$10, add $3;
$10.01-$25, add $5; $25.01-$50, add $6; $50.01-$75, add $7;
$75.01-$150, add $8; $150.01 or more, add $10.

At your Bookdealer or direct from the Publisher.
Toll Free 1-800-437-5876   **Fax 815-226-7770**

MARY FABYAN WINDEATT

Mary Fabyan Windeatt could well be called the "storyteller of the saints," for such indeed she was. And she had a singular talent for bringing out doctrinal truths in her stories, so that without even realizing it, young readers would see the Catholic catechism come to life in the lives of the saints.

Mary Fabyan Windeatt wrote at least 21 books for children, plus the text of about 28 Catholic story coloring books. At one time there were over 175,000 copies of her books on the saints in circulation. She contributed a regular "Children's Page" to the monthly Dominican magazine, *The Torch*.

Miss Windeatt began her career of writing for the Catholic press around age 24. After graduating from San Diego State College in 1934, she had gone to New York looking for work in advertising. Not finding any, she sent a story to a Catholic magazine. It was accepted—and she continued to write. Eventually Miss Windeatt wrote for 33 magazines, contributing verse, articles, book reviews and short stories.

Having been born in 1910 in Regina, Saskatchewan, Canada, Mary Fabyan Windeatt received the Licentiate of Music degree from Mount Saint Vincent College in Halifax, Nova Scotia at age 17. With her family she moved to San Diego in that same year, 1927. In 1940 Miss Windeatt received an A.M. degree from Columbia University. Later, she lived with her mother near St. Meinrad's Abbey, St. Meinrad, Indiana. Mary Fabyan Windeatt died on November 20, 1979.

(Much of the above information is from Catholic Authors: Contemporary Biographical Sketches 1930-1947, *ed. by Matthew Hoehn, O.S.B., B.L.S., St. Mary's Abbey, Newark, N.J., 1957.)*